AAT

Qualifications and Credit Framework (QCF)
LEVEL 4 DIPLOMA IN ACCOUNTING

WORKBOOK

Internal Control and
Accounting Systems

2012 Edition

First edition July 2010

Third edition June 2012

ISBN 9781 4453 9499 2
(Previous edition: 9780 7517 9775 6)

British Library Cataloguing-in-Publication Data
A catalogue record for this book is available from the British
Library

Published by

BPP Learning Media Ltd
BPP House
Aldine Place
London
W12 8AA

www.bpp.com/learningmedia

Printed in the United Kingdom

Your learning materials, published by BPP Learning Media Ltd,
are printed on paper sourced from sustainable, managed forests.

CONTENTS

BPP LEARNING MEDIA'S AAT MATERIALS

Since July 2010 the AAT's assessments have fallen within the **Qualifications and Credit Framework** and most papers are now assessed by way of an on demand **computer based assessment**. BPP Learning Media has invested heavily to ensure our ground breaking materials are as relevant as possible for this method of assessment. In particular, our **suite of online resources** ensures that you are prepared for online testing by allowing you to practise numerous online tasks that are similar to the tasks you will encounter in the AAT's assessments.

The BPP range of resources comprises:

- **Texts**, covering all the knowledge and understanding needed by students, with numerous illustrations of 'how it works', practical examples and tasks for you to use to consolidate your learning. The majority of tasks within the texts have been written in an interactive style that reflects the style of the online tasks we anticipate the AAT will set. Texts are available in our traditional paper format and, in addition, as ebooks which can be downloaded to your PC or laptop.

- **Question Banks**, including additional learning questions plus the AAT's practice assessment and a number of other full practice assessments. Full answers to all questions and assessments, prepared by BPP Learning Media Ltd, are included. Our question banks are provided free of charge in an online environment containing tasks similar to those you will encounter in the AAT's testing environment. This means you can become familiar with being tested in an online environment prior to completing the real assessment.

- **Passcards**, which are handy pocket-sized revision tools designed to fit in a handbag or briefcase to enable you to revise anywhere at anytime. All major points are covered in the Passcards which have been designed to assist you in consolidating knowledge.

- **Workbooks**, which have been designed to cover the units that are assessed by way of project/case study. The workbooks contain many practical tasks to assist in the learning process and also a sample assessment or project to work through.

- **Lecturers' resources**, providing a further bank of tasks, answers and full practice assessments for classroom use, available separately only to lecturers whose colleges adopt BPP Learning Media material. The practice assessments within the lecturers' resources are available in both paper format and online in e format.

This Workbook for *Internal Control and Accounting Systems* has been written to specifically to ensure comprehensive yet concise coverage of the new assessment criteria. It is fully up to date as at June 2012 and reflects both the AAT's study guide and the practice assessment provided by the AAT.

This edition of BPP's Workbook for the AAT Level 4 Diploma in Accounting paper – Internal Control and Accounting Systems, has been carefully designed to enable students to practise all aspects of the requirements of the Standards of Competence and Learning Outcomes of the two units; Principles of Internal Control and Evaluating Accounting Systems, and **to** ultimately produce a successful project that demonstrates their competence.

The chapters contain these key features:

- clear, step by step explanation of the topic

- clear guidance on how to produce a professional management report and an explanation of the key contents of one

- logical progression and linking from one chapter to the next

- practical guidance on completion of each section based on the organisation chosen

- Case Study advice at the end of each chapter for students completing this project using the AAT Case Study Scenario

- The AAT practice case study and specimen report.

If you have any comments about this book, please e-mail paulsutcliffe@bpp.com or write to Paul Sutcliffe, Senior Publishing Manager, BPP Learning Media Ltd, BPP House, Aldine Place, London W12 8AA.

STANDARDS OF COMPETENCE

LEARNING OUTCOMES OF ICAS

This paper is made up of two units under the new Qualifications and Curriculum Framework (QCF) – Principles of Internal Control, a knowledge based unit, and Evaluating Accounting Systems which is skills based.

One purpose of these units is to ensure that learners know and understand the role of accounting in an organisation, and why internal controls should be in place.

Another is to ensure that learners are able to communicate clearly in writing, at a level 4 standard and in a manner appropriate to the workplace.

The knowledge unit aims are to ensure that learners understand the principles of internal control. It has set learning outcomes so that learners are able to identify the role of accounting in general, and internal controls specifically, within an organisation. They must be able to make informed reasoned judgements to inform management on how to implement or improve systems within an organisation. The 3 learning outcomes of this unit are:

- Demonstrate an understanding of the role of accounting within the organisation.

- Understand the importance and use of internal control systems

- Be able to identify and use the appropriate accounting system to meet specific organisational requirements.

The skills unit aims to ensure that learners can evaluate accounting systems within an organisation and consider whether they are appropriate to that organisation or not. They should be able to identify the organisation's accounting system requirements, explain where improvements could be made and make valid suggestions about how to do this through communicating their recommendations to management in a clear manner, supported by reasoned argument. They should also be able to identify the impact that changes would have on the system and its users. The two learning outcomes of this unit are:

- Evaluate the accounting system and identify areas for improvement
- Make recommendations to improve the accounting system

Each of the learning outcomes above has a number of assessment criteria attached to it, that learners will need to demonstrate competence in to complete this paper.

The AAT have also published, in unit guides, set guidance on the requirements of each of the assessment criteria.

Each chapter in this companion is mapped to the learning outcomes and assessment criteria below.

Principles of Internal Control and Evaluating Accounting Systems

Paper Commentary

This paper is about your ability to review accounting systems, and their appropriateness to a chosen organisation, including the internal controls in place.

The first unit requires you to show that you understand the role of accounting within the organisation, identify the accounting system appropriate to meet the organisations requirements and to understand the importance and use of internal control systems.

The second unit is about evaluating the accounting system, identifying areas for improvement and making appropriate recommendations to improve it.

Learning Outcomes contained within this unit are:

Principles of Internal Control:

- Demonstrate an understanding of the role of accounting within the organisation.
- Understand the importance and use of internal control systems
- Be able to identify and use the appropriate accounting system to meet specific organisational requirements.

Evaluating Accounting Systems:

- Evaluate the accounting system and identify areas for improvement
- Make recommendations to improve the accounting system

Assessment Criteria

Principles of Internal Control (PIC)		
Learning Outcome	**Assessment Criteria**	**Chapter**
1. Demonstrate an understanding of the role of accounting within the organisation	**1.1** Describe the purpose, structure and organisation of the accounting function and its relationships with other functions within the organisation	**Chapter 3**
	1.2 Explain the various business purposes for which the following financial information is required ■ Income statement ■ Forecast of statement of cash flows ■ Statement of financial position	**Chapter 4**
	1.3 Give an overview of the organisation's business and its critical external relationships with stakeholders	**Chapter 2**
	1.4 Explain how the accounting systems are affected by the organisational structure, systems, procedures, and business transactions	**Chapters 3, 4**
	1.5 Explain the effect on users of changes to accounting systems caused by ■ External regulations ■ Organisational policies and procedures	**Chapter 2**

Principles of Internal Control (PIC)		
Learning Outcome	**Assessment Criteria**	**Chapter**
2. Understand the importance and use of internal control systems	**2.1** Identify the external regulations that affect accounting practice	**Chapter 2**
	2.2 Describe the causes of, and common types of, fraud and the impact of this on the organisation	**Chapter 6**
	2.3 Explain methods that can be used to detect fraud within an accounting system	**Chapters 5, 6**
	2.4 Explain the types of controls that can be put in place to ensure compliance with statutory or organisational requirements	**Chapters 5, 6**
3. Be able to identify and use the appropriate accounting system to meet specific organisational requirements	**3.1** Identify weaknesses in accounting systems ■ Potential for errors ■ Exposure to possible fraud.	**Chapters 4, 6**
	3.2 Explain how an accounting system can support internal control	**Chapters 4, 5**
	3.3 Identify ways of supporting individuals who operate accounting systems using ■ Training ■ Manuals ■ Written information ■ Help menus	**Chapter 4**
	3.4 Explain the value and benefit to a specific organisation of different types of accounting systems and software packages	**Chapters 4, 7**

Evaluating Accounting Systems (EAS)		
Learning Outcome	**Assessment Criteria**	**Chapter**
1. Evaluate the accounting system and identify areas for improvement	**1.1** Identify an organisation's accounting system requirements	**Chapter 3**
	1.2 Review record keeping systems to confirm whether they meet the organisation's requirements for financial information	**Chapter 4**
	1.3 Identify weaknesses in and the potential for improvements to, the accounting system and consider their impact on the operation of the organisation	**Chapter 4**
	1.4 Identify potential areas of fraud arising from lack of control within the accounting system and grade the risk	**Chapter 6**
	1.5 Review methods of operating for cost effectiveness, reliability and speed	**Chapters 4, 7**
2. Make recommendations to improve the accounting system	**2.1** Make recommendations for changes to the accounting system in an easily understood format, with a clear rationale and an explanation of any assumptions made.	**Chapter 7**
	2.2 Identify the effects that any recommended changes would have on the users of the system.	**Chapters 4, 6 & 7**
	2.3 Enable individuals who operate accounting systems to understand how to use the system to fulfil their responsibilities.	**Chapters 4, 6 & 7**

Evaluating Accounting Systems (EAS)		
Learning Outcome	**Assessment Criteria**	**Chapter**
	2.4 Identify the implications of recommended changes in terms of time, financial costs, benefits, and operating procedures.	**Chapter 7**

ASSESSMENT STRATEGY

The assessment will take the form of a formal report written by the learner and assessed locally by the training provider. The report can be based upon the workplace of the student, or upon a scenario provided by AAT through LearnPlus as a computer-based project (CBP).

The project takes the form of a report to management that analyses the accounting system within the organisation, assessing whether it is appropriate. It should specifically address the appropriateness of internal controls and make recommendations to improve both the system itself and the controls within it. In producing this report students will need to prove competence in their ability to review an organisation and its accounting systems, and an understanding of internal controls for different organisation types.

The report should be approximately 4000 words long and should provide good analysis and an in depth review of one part of the accounting system of an organisation. It must cover all the assessment criteria for both units.

The AAT has provided the following guidance on the required presentation and content of the report. We are grateful to the AAT for permitting us to reproduce this.

The report should be **presented** as follows:

- Written in the third person, that is to say not using any personal pronouns (for example: I, me, he or she).

- Spelling and grammar of a suitable level for a business report at Level 4, which is degree level standard.

- Word processed.

- The report must be numbered by section and paragraph number and mapped to the assessment.

- The report should show a 'reasonable' level of literacy skills. Whilst it would be unfair to penalise a candidate with a not yet competent decision for one spelling mistake, or the occasional use of a personal pronoun, overall the report should be fit for publication to the management of a company.

- The report should not be written in bullet point style, but should be well detailed and written in depth. Bullet points should only be used as listing, with each point then analysed.

The **content** of the report should include:

- A review of the current accounting systems, focusing on record keeping systems, principles of internal control, current methods of fraud prevention, and working methods and training.

    - An analysis of the above.

- An identification of weaknesses or areas where improvement could be made.

    - Each weakness should be analysed and explained in depth, including the effect it has upon the organisation and/or staff.

- Recommendations to improve the accounting system.

    - Each recommendation should be analysed and explained in depth, including the effect it has upon the organisation and/or staff

- A cost-benefit analysis.

- Financial figures must be placed in the report, even if they are 'guesstimates'. It is not sufficient to say 'a large amount of money will be saved' or 'there are no costs associated with this recommendation as only staff time is used'.

    - Candidates should be encouraged to use assumptions, and these should be accepted as long as they are realistic. For example, assuming the salary of the finance director is £80,000 per annum then a saving of £8,000 can be assumed. This is realistic even if you know they earn £100,000. However if the student had put that figure as a monthly salary then this could be considered as not being realistic.

The assessment material (CBP) will be delivered online and assessed locally. The local assessor (training provider) will be required to ensure that all assessment criteria are covered. Learners will be required to demonstrate competence across the assessment criteria for this learning and assessment area.

The AAT also set out the following respective responsibilities of the learner and the assessor in their guidance on writing the report (available at www.aat.org.uk at the time of publication of this workbook).

Responsibilities as a learner:

- Identify the theme for your report
- Meet with the assessor at agreed times
- Draft the report
- Map to the assessment criteria
- Present the final report
- Keep your assessor informed on progress
- Stick to target dates and deadlines

Responsibilities as an assessor:

- Schedule the assessment
- Agree the theme of the report
- Give guidance on the draft report
- Give additional assessment opportunities as necessary
- Assess the final report
- Hold an assessment interview if necessary

Duration of assessment

Note: The following information is taken from the AAT guidance for ICAS provided by the AAT at the date of publishing (June 2012).

The amount of teaching input will of course vary between training providers, but it is expected that once teaching has been completed, the report will be written and completed as follows.

AAT assessment

- For the first submission, learners must submit a substantial report for formal assessment within four months* of the scheduled assessment start date.

- After reviewing the leaner's first submission (substantial report) the assessor may permit the learner up to four further opportunities to submit additional supporting evidence. Additional submissions of evidence should be complete within six months* of the scheduled assessment start date or at the discretion of the assessor.

* For learners with reasonable adjustment and special consideration (RASC)
please view the AAT RASC policy available online.

Workplace evidence and recognition of prior learning

Deadline setting for workplace evidence and recognition of prior learning is at the discretion of the assessor. A maximum of five submissions are allowed.

HOW TO USE THIS WORKBOOK

This workbook contains tasks for you, the student, to complete. By completing these tasks, and then reviewing the suggested solutions, you are learning about organisations, their accounting systems and their internal controls. These are the areas that make up the standards of competence, learning outcomes and assessment criteria of this paper.

You should work through the book taking each chapter in turn; stopping and thinking about each of the tasks presented to you. If you are in a class at a training provider, your tutor may ask you to discuss a task and see how many answers a group of you can come up with before reviewing them with you. If you are studying on your own then you might like to jot down as many ideas as you can, perhaps using the Internet to help you, before looking at the suggested answers.

At the end of each chapter there is an explanation of how to complete the relevant section of your report based on what you have covered in the chapter. This should be supplemented by advice from your tutor and/or assessor and you should ensure that you let your assessor see your work as you progress so that they can provide you with appropriate advice and feedback.

chapter 1:
THE BASIC PRINCIPLES OF ICAS

chapter coverage 📖

In this chapter we will look at the basic principles of the two units that make up this paper – Internal Controls and Accounting Systems (ICAS):

✍ Principles of Internal Controls (IC)

✍ Evaluating Accounting Systems (EAS)

We will review the learning outcomes of the two units and how to ensure that they are covered within the management report you are required to write in order to demonstrate competence in the standards.

We will also review the Assessment Process so that you are aware of the demands on both you the student and your assessor in order that competence be demonstrated and assessed.

We will also discuss a critical question when considering how to write the required report – should you base this around the organisation in which you work or an AAT Case Study? If you wish to complete it based on your own organisation there are certain factors to consider which we will review.

We will also review the approach to the ICAS report for students for whom English is not their first language and where you may be able to access additional advice and support if this relates to you.

Finally we will review some Frequently Asked Questions (FAQs) from this unit to (hopefully!) address any concerns that you may have on how to complete it.

THE ICAS MANAGEMENT REPORT

The ICAS project should be presented to your assessor as a report to management, with appropriate appendices. It must be written in a professional business style, and analyse the learning outcomes identified in each of the two units that make up this paper. These are:

Principles of Internal Control:

- Demonstrate an understanding of the role of accounting within the organisation.
- Understand the importance and use of internal control systems.
- Be able to identify and use the appropriate accounting system to meet specific organisational requirements.

Evaluating Accounting Systems:

- Evaluate the accounting system and identify areas for improvement
- Make recommendations to improve the accounting system

This report can either be based on the organisation where you work or on an AAT written Case Study that your assessor can provide you with.

The report should be approximately 4,000 words in length (excluding your appendices); however this is only a guide. You and your assessor should ensure that your work covers all of the standards required in this unit in order that it be assessed as competent.

If your work is significantly under this count then it probably does not contain all the areas required. Map it carefully to the assessment criteria (see Chapter 7) and ensure all are covered sufficiently. If your finished report is much longer than this then it may be too wordy or you may have more in it than required. Ask your assessor for advice and ensure that your word count does *not* include your appendices.

The report must also be written in an appropriate format and include certain sections. The final version, which **must be word processed**, might include:

- Title Page
- Contents
- Terms of Reference
- Executive Summary
- Methodology
- Introduction to the Organisation
- The Accounts Department
- A Review of the Accounting System
- Internal Control and an Analysis of Fraud
- Recommendations to Improve
- Cost Benefit Analysis
- Appendices

This workbook will take you through the key areas of the report, explaining each in detail, and how to achieve competence in them. It will also guide you through the compilation of the report and the sections required to be in it and why.

It will then explain to you how to map your work to the standards and ensure all areas are covered. In each section it explains which standards must be covered and gives guidance and support on how to do this.

Once you are a fully qualified AAT Technician an employer would expect you to be able to produce a professional management report in an appropriate style and format. By the time you have completed this unit these are the skills and knowledge you will have gained.

OWN ORGANISATION OR CASE STUDY?

Own organisation

If you work in an organisation where you can investigate whether the accounting systems and controls in place are appropriate to the organisation, and report to management on them, then this is the best approach to take. This will not only mean you produce a good report that is competent but also that you have added value to your organisation and ensured your recommendations are noted by management.

You may be thinking that your organisation is too large or too controlled by management for any of your recommendations to be implemented - this does not matter. Implementation of any recommendations made is not a requirement of this unit.

The main outcome of your work should be that you have investigated the accounting systems and the internal controls in place within it and made recommendations for improvement. By having done this you will have gained a great deal of knowledge about your work place and this can only enhance your value to your organisation.

You may also be thinking that there are no improvements to be made, perhaps your workplace is already perfect! It is usual that after further research some improvements can be identified – again, we stress that they do not have to be implemented. If, however, you complete your research and find that there are no recommendations to make then this is acceptable (though very rare!). As long as in your detailed report you have covered all the learning outcomes in sufficient detail then your work should be assessed as competent.

Note that in order to complete this work based on your work place you will require your **manager's approval**. They will need to sign an **authenticity statement** once you have presented them with your final report to testify that it is based on the work place and is a true representation of it.

Your manager will also be required to testify that the work is your own, unaided and that your recommendations have been discussed with them orally. You must have their approval to do this, as without this statement your assessor can not assess your work.

If, after consideration, you find that you are unable to investigate all the learning outcomes in your own organisation then you may find that the Case Study is for you.

It may be the case that your employer does not know you are studying or that you are not working in an accounting role and therefore you are not able to investigate and report on an accounting system. If this is the case then the AAT Case Study scenario may be more appropriate for you.

Case Study

In completing your work based on the Case Study you will need to ensure that it reads as if you work in the organisation described in the case study. Your final report should be no different to that of a student who is writing based on their own organisation.

The AAT will present the Case Study to you in an electronic format via the AAT e portfolio system. It will consist of several documents describing a fictitious organisation, its accounts department and its staff.

You must read through the entire Case Study and assume all the information contained within it is your own knowledge of the work place.

You should complete each section of your report on the assumption that your assessor has no prior knowledge of the organisation.

Your assessor will take the place of the work place manager and must produce an authenticity statement at the end once competence has been achieved. In order that they can do this, you will need to provide them with drafts of your work so that they can give advice, support and feedback but also be assured it is your own and unaided work. You must be in constant contact with them throughout the process.

Case Study Advice

This Workbook features specific advice within each chapter on how to use the Case Study to complete your work. Look out for the paragraphs formatted like this.

If you do select to complete your report based on an AAT Case Study then be aware that once you have access to the scenario on the AAT's e portfolio system you will then have to submit a report for formal assessment within four months of the scheduled assessment start date. During those four months you are permitted to have up to five 'formative guidance meetings' with your tutor where you can receive guidance on your progress to date.

BPP LEARNING MEDIA

Having reviewed your first submission, if your assessor assesses you as 'not yet competent', then you may have four further opportunities to submit more supporting evidence (at the discretion of the assessor). Submissions of additional evidence should be completed within six months of the scheduled assessment start date or at the discretion of the assessor.

Note: The time limits, the number of times reports/evidence may be submitted and the assessment guidance included in this chapter are based on the AAT guidance in force at the time this book was published (June 2012). You should check these details with your assessor and read the latest AAT guidance to ensure that you are aware of any changes to the assessment guidance following publication of this workbook.

ASSESSMENT STANDARDS

The ICAS project is assessed once completed by the student. As part of the assessment process the assessor is required to confirm that the work meets the following criteria (VACS):

- **Valid** – it meets the standards

- **Authentic** – it is the student's own, unaided work

- **Current** – it has been written recently and reflects how the organisation currently operates

- **Sufficient** – it investigates the key areas in sufficient detail to meet the standards

Its **validity** is assured by the student mapping the work to the learning outcomes. This means that you must cross-reference all your work to the criteria of this unit. To do this you must number all the pages and paragraphs of your work and write the relevant paragraph number into a mapping document next to the criteria they refer to.

Authenticity is assured by the student and the assessor working together through the project. This process starts with the student submitting a proposal to the assessor, which the assessor feeds back on. Your assessor should then review drafts of your work as you progress and provide further feedback on this. This aids them in being sure your work is your own and unaided. It is worth also noting that they may not be able to authenticate work that is presented to them as a fully completed report where they have not seen and fed back on drafts as they were written.

For students completing this report based on their work place they then require a signed and dated statement, on company headed paper, from their manager testifying that the work is their own, unaided and a true reflection of the work place. If this can not be obtained then the Case Study would be a better option for the student.

For Case Study students the assessor will act as their manager. In this situation the assessor will sign and date a witness statement to the same effect as the work place manager above. It is even more critical that for Case Study reports the student submits drafts and the assessor feeds back on them.

Authenticity may also be confirmed through a final interview between the student and the assessor once the work has been submitted and assessed. In the final interview the assessor asks the student questions about the work they have completed. This enables them to confirm the work is their own and unaided. The final interview may also be used by the assessor to strengthen any weaker areas of the learning outcomes and assessment criteria.

Currency concerns whether the report is up-to-date and relevant in the work place. It is worth remembering this and ensuring your work is assessed as soon as possible after its completion. Many students start this project and then do not complete it for some time, possibly years, later. This may mean that their work is no longer current and so a new project would have to be written.

Sufficiency relates to the work covering the learning outcomes in sufficient detail for the assessor to be sure that it meets the standards required. For some of the assessment criteria it may be necessary to include technical notes in the appendices of your report, to explain a point fully, as you have not been able to do this in the body of your report. This is acceptable and your assessor should be able to advise you on this.

THE ASSESSMENT PROCESS

The assessment process has already been discussed in this chapter but it is important that you, the student, understand it fully so that you can ensure you complete your work appropriately, get it assessed promptly and complete this unit and your level 4 Diploma.

The first stage of the process is that the assessor should discuss the project with you and review your initial ideas. This is a **project proposal** and can either be done through you submitting a formal written document or in a one to one discussion with your assessor. Either way a documented record of this must be kept as it might be reviewed by the AAT once competence has been achieved.

The assessor may, at this stage, agree with you an **assessment plan.** This should cover how the report will be completed and a timescale. It should include a plan as to when each draft will be submitted for feedback and when the final version will be ready.

The assessment plan is just that – a plan. It will be revised and updated as the project progresses and again is a key part of the document audit trail required by the AAT for this unit.

Once the approach to the report has been agreed then **drafts** should be submitted to your assessor for review and formative guidance in the form of feedback. This ensures that you keep on the right track as you complete the work and that the assessor can be sure your work is your own and unaided.

Do not complete too much of the report before submitting it. Any assessor might be suspicious of a fully completed report being handed in for assessment if they have not worked with and guided the student through its completion.

Your assessor can only provide you with a maximum of five formative guidance sessions and / or written feedback so you should ensure that you address their comments within your report after each session.

Your assessor should explain to you at the start of this paper's completion exactly how and in what format this formative guidance will take place.

One of the requirements the AAT place on assessors is that they ensure you have **mapped your work to the required criteria.** This is covered in detail in Chapter 7; for now it is important to understand that your work will not be accepted without this mapping. It must be mapped to all the learning outcomes in order that it can be assessed.

Once a **final version** of your report is ready then it must be **professionally presented** and submitted for assessment. It must be submitted with your **manager's authenticity statement** (if completing the report on your workplace) and with your full mapping to the standards. It must include all the formatting requirements discussed later in this Workbook and all the required sections, *each starting on a new page.*

The assessor then undertakes a formal assessment of the work. They do this in a number of different ways and are, in essence, confirming the VACS criteria discussed earlier in this chapter. This is then documented and fed back to you.

The final stage of the assessment process for this unit then takes place once the assessor has assessed the work to the VACS criteria. This might take the format of a **final interview** which takes place between the student and the assessor to discuss the work, its completion and key outcomes.

The assessor can also use the final interview to ask questions regarding any areas of the learning outcomes that were weak in the final report. This gives them a small amount of flexibility in their assessment although it would not be expected that this be used to assess to sufficient detail the key areas of the report. It is used more to test and probe further a point and this aids them in confirming the authenticity of the work.

Then the assessor submits the work for **Internal Moderation (IM)**. This is an internal quality assurance system required by all such qualifications.

The centre IM checks a sample of all assessors' work in order to confirm that it is to standard and to provide appropriate feedback and support. Although it would not be expected that the assessor's decision of competence be overturned as a result of this, it could happen and you could be asked to amend your work or update it.

Again, it is rare that the overall assessment decision be overturned but this does, on occasion, occur. If this is the case your assessor will contact you with information about the additional work required for competence.

Once this period has passed, or your work is scrutinised and accepted, your provisional result will then be updated.

As highlighted earlier in this Chapter, one thing to note is that at the assessor's discretion, you may have further opportunities to submit additional supporting evidence if you are initially assessed as not competent (following your first submission of a substantial report for formal assessment).

The assessment process

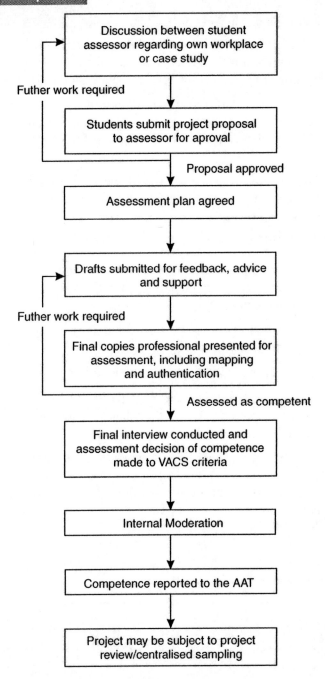

Discussion between student
assessor regarding own workplace
or case study

Futher work required

Students submit project proposal
to assessor for aproval

Proposal approved

Assessment plan agreed

Drafts submitted for feedback, advice
and support

Futher work required

Final copies professional presented for
assessment, including mapping
and authentication

Assessed as competent

Final interview conducted and
assessment decision of competence
made to VACS criteria

Internal Moderation

Competence reported to the AAT

Project may be subject to project
review/centralised sampling

THE AAT LEARNING OUTCOMES AND STANDARDS OF COMPETENCE

The AAT standards of competence (or syllabus), consisting of learning outcomes and assessment criteria, are the areas that you have to show competence in, in order to demonstrate that you can perform the duties and tasks required.

To complete a paper successfully you must demonstrate competence in all of the standards of competence. The AAT also publish guidance on how each of the standards of competence can be met. This can be found in the unit guides on their website.

A full set of the standards of competence, plus guidance on which chapter of this companion covers them, is included in the introduction to this companion.

Case Study Advice

If you are completing a report based on the AAT Case Study, your assessor will take the place of your work place manager and testify that your work is your own, unaided and authentic.

It is critical therefore that you submit a proposal and drafts to them as your work progresses and get feedback.

This aids your assessor in confirming your work is authentic.

If you have a Case Study but have not yet completed the report and want it to be assessed by a different assessor, contact them first. Do not complete the report and then submit it.

There is a possibility that the assessor will ask you to start again as they cannot be sure of the authenticity of your work. Remember that under the ICAS assessment rules you only have four months from the scheduled assessment start date to submit a report for formal assessment. The initial assessment may be a 'not yet competent' decision as further work is required, but you may still have opportunities to submit additional evidence to demonstrate competency. However, if you do not meet the AAT deadlines then you may be required to start your work again on an alternative scenario.

THE ICAS PROJECT FOR STUDENTS FOR WHOM ENGLISH IS NOT THEIR FIRST LANGUAGE

The AAT qualification is an English language-based qualification and to complete it you will be required to demonstrate an ability to write a professional report – in English. If English is not your first language this may prove difficult for you. There are several practical things you can do:

(a) Talk to your assessor – they will be able to advise and support you (but note they can not proof read or correct your work for you)

(b) Ask a friend or colleague to be a mentor – they are able to proof read your work and advise you on any amendments that can be made

(c) Turn on your spellchecker – the finished report needs to be typed so complete it using a word processing package with the spellchecker and grammar checker turned on to highlight any errors made

(d) Contact your AAT members' society – they may be able to provide you with an AAT member volunteer who can proof read your work and advise you on the completion of it

Your assessor must be confident that your finished and final report is professional and in good business English. They can not report it as competent unless it is. If you need help and support to do this then raise this as early as possible in the process.

FAQS

1 **What areas must my project cover?** – The analysis of an accounting system, a review of internal controls and the opportunity for fraudulent activities, recommendations to improve the system and a cost benefit analysis of the recommendations. An example of the sections you could include were covered earlier in this chapter.

2 **Does this have to be based on my work place?** – No, the AAT produce a Case Study on which you may base your report but in this case it should look no different to a report based on a real organisation. To complete it you will have to assume you work in the organisation and all the information contained in the scenario is knowledge you have obtained from working there. An AAT written sample Case Study, and a sample completed report, are included in the back of this workbook.

3 **How long should the finished report be?** – Approximately 4,000 words; however you must cover all the learning outcomes and lay the report out in a certain format so if you are significantly under or over this amount talk to your assessor for advice.

4 **Should I write the whole report then submit it for assessment?** – No. This is dangerous as your assessor must be sure your work is authentic and if you do this they will be unable to be sure. Also it is very difficult to produce a perfect report first time.

Submit a proposal and drafts to your assessor and get feedback and support as your complete your work. This will not only make the process easier for you but ensure they are comfortable that your work is your own.

5 **My English is not very good – will this affect my competence?** – It could do, yes. Your final report must be in English and be in a professional written style. See the section in this chapter on students for whom English is not their first language for advice and support on how to ensure your work is to an acceptable standard.

6 **Must my project cover all the learning outcomes?** – Yes. In order to be judged competent you must cover all the criteria sufficiently. See the chapters on the assessment process and mapping to assist you in doing this.

7 **I completed a project some time ago but it was never assessed, can I now submit it for assessment?** – As the standards of this unit have now changed from the NVQ / Diploma unit 10 you will need to review and discuss this with your assessor and additional work will be required. Your assessor must ensure that the original work is still valid (eg that your recommendations to improve the system are still relevant for) and authentic – your own, unaided work. They may not be able to assess your work and may ask that you start again based on your work place or a Case Study.

8 **My manager won't or can't produce an authentication statement, what can I do?** – If you have completed your project on your work place and your manager will not produce an appropriate authenticity statement, signed and dated on company headed paper, you do not have permission to submit your project based on your place of work. Without this statement your assessor may not be able to assess your work and so you would be asked to start your project again, perhaps based on a Case Study. It is important therefore that you gain your manager's consent before commencing your project using your own work place. If you are unable to obtain a manager's authentication statement you must let your assessor know as soon as possible. They may be able to provide a statement if they are confident the work is your own and there is a valid reason for not obtaining a statement (such as the manager being ill).

9 **I am completing my project using the Case Study, who is my work place manager and how can they authenticate my work?** – When you complete the project based on the scenario in the Case Study your assessor takes on the role of work place manager and as part of the assessment process they will produce an authenticity statement. It is vital therefore that you submit a proposal and drafts of your work as you complete it so that they are able to testify that the work is your own and unaided.

10 **What is an assessment plan and must I complete one?** – An assessment plan is the result of a negotiation between you and your assessor to plan when and how you are going to complete each phase of the project and submit a final version of your work. It is an invaluable tool to carefully plan how you can complete the overall report. You do not need to keep exactly to the plan, it can be reviewed and updated as you progress.

11 **What is a project proposal and must I complete one?** – A project proposal is where you set out to your assessor your initial thoughts and ideas regarding your project. It is vital as it ensures that your assessor can judge whether your project will be appropriate and that you are not proposing too large or small an area of the accounting system to investigate. It allows your assessor to provide you with valuable feedback and support and is a key part of the authentication process.

12 **What is the final interview and what format will it take?** – The final interview is the last part of the assessment process and is where the assessor asks you questions about the work you have produced. It can aid them in authenticating your work and strengthen any minor areas of weakness so that they can be sure of the sufficiency of your competence. It should take the format of an interview, where your assessor will ask you questions and you provide answers. It will be recorded – either written down or voice recorded – and if written you will be asked to confirm that the written evidence is a true reflection of the interview by signing and dating it. A final interview is not required for every student and your assessor will decide whether it is required in your case.

13 **How do I map my work and why must I do so?** – Mapping your work is where you inform the assessor of the page and paragraph number that covers each of the learning outcomes. This is important first, so that you can be sure that all the criteria are covered (if you can't map to one of them then you have missed it out and need to add a paragraph to include it!) and also to ensure that you have a good understanding of what you have gained competence in, by producing this work. To map your work take a copy of the learning outcomes and assessment criteria (see earlier) and reference each page and paragraph number to them.

14 **Can my project be a series of paragraphs, each addressing the learning outcomes in turn?** – No. This is not an appropriate way to produce a professional management report and would not be judged as competent as you will have not demonstrated an ability to write one. Instead, your report should be structured around the sections as outlined in this workbook

15 **What is Internal Verification / Moderation?** – This is an internal quality assurance check. Each AAT Approved Assessment Centre has an internal verifier or moderator who is responsible for ensuring that work reported to the AAT as competent has been appropriately assessed and is actually competent. They do this through a variety of processes and you may have your assessed work reviewed or your final interview observed. If they do not agree with an assessment decision this will be communicated to you either by the AAT directly or your assessor and the additional work required to achieve competence will be discussed.

16 **I can not see how to include all the assessment criteria and learning outcomes in my report – what do I do?** – First of all you should discuss this with your assessor. They will review the mapping you have completed and also they understand the technical requirements of the standards. They will advise you but you should remember that if you are unable to cover all the assessment criteria fully and sufficiently in the body of your report you can include technical notes in the appendices to supplement and strengthen them. This should only be by exception however and not the rule and your assessor is best placed to advise you on this.

17 **What is formative guidance and why is it limited?** – under the AAT rules of assessment of this unit there is a maximum of five formative guidance feedbacks that can be provided to you by your assessor. This may be in the form of meetings or written feedback with or from your assessor. In each case your assessor should review the work you have completed to date and provide you with guidance on how it should be amended and what to complete next. This is limited to a maximum of five sessions to ensure that the work completed is your own and not as a result of too much assessor input. If, after five guidance sessions, your work is still not ready for assessment then your assessor may advise you that you are not yet ready to complete this unit and that you should undertake further development before attempting it again.

18 **What is assessment and why is it limited?** – under the AAT rules of assessment in this unit, in addition to the five maximum formative guidance sessions, your assessor can then undertake a maximum number of assessments as specified by the AAT. **You should check the guidance provided by the AAT to see what the current maximum is.** At the time of writing this book, the assessor may permit a student up to four further opportunities to submit additional evidence following the initial submission. If, after these additional submissions, your work is still not yet competent it may be that your assessor advises you that you are not yet ready to complete this unit and that you need to undertake further development before attempting it again.

19 **How long do I have to complete my report?** – if you are completing the report on an AAT Case Study then you have up to four months from the assessment start date to submit your report. Once this period has elapsed you may find access to the scenario blocked such that you will need to start this unit again on an alternative one. If you are completing this report in your workplace, your assessor will advise you of the time constraints in place; they are likely to be similar. If you do not complete your report within these time limits then you may be required to start this unit again.

chapter 2:
INTRODUCTION TO THE ORGANISATION

chapter coverage 📖

This chapter covers some of the learning outcomes from the unit; Principles of Internal Control. Within it we will be looking at various types of organisation and the differences between them. We will then look at organisation structure as there are many different structure types and these will influence the organisation's culture and how it operates

Organisations are also influenced by the stakeholders in the organisation – these are groups who are in some way affected by the organisation's actions. Stakeholder groups include employees, customers, suppliers and the community within which the organisation exists. Stakeholders can be categorised as either internal or external groups and we will look at how the organisation must react to the changing needs and demands of these groups.

Finally we will look at the regulatory framework within which the organisation exists and the impact that this will have on it.

The last section of this chapter will then explain how to include all of the above in your report, and to ensure that you explain them in relation to the organisation you have chosen to analyse, whether your own or an AAT Case Study.

ASSESSMENT CRITERIA

PIC 1.3 – Give an overview of the organisation's business and its critical external relationships with stakeholders

PIC 1.5 – Explain the effect on users of changes to accounting systems caused by:

- External regulations
- Organisational policies and procedures

PIC 2.1 – Identify the external regulations that affect accounting practice

ORGANISATION TYPES

There are many different types of organisation, most of which you can choose to base your ICAS report on. You should be able to identify these different types and recognise which your chosen organisation is and why that affects how it is structured and how it operates.

Most organisation types can be grouped into two distinct sectors:

- The public sector
- The private sector

And each of these sectors consists of a range of organisations who have different, distinct characteristics.

The public sector

Organisations operating within the public sector include central government, local government and businesses owned by the government. An example of a business owned by the government would be NHS Direct. The number of businesses owned by the government (often known as Nationalised Businesses) has shrunk considerably over the last 25 years, however, the recent banking crisis did see the government taking all or part ownership of a number of UK Banks.

Public sector organisations typically have very different objectives to those in the private sector as they are often responsible for providing a service rather than selling a product. For example, local government is responsible for many services including:

- Waste collection and disposal
- Street lighting
- Library services
- Museums
- Paths and parks
- Licensing

The private sector

Organisations in the private sector include the following:

- Sole traders
- Partnerships
- Private limited companies (Ltd
- Public limited companies (plc)

They primarily exist to make profits for the owners, through the provision of goods and services to paying customers.

Sole traders and partnerships differ from limited companies because their liability is unlimited. Unlimited liability means that the owners are personally liable for all of the debts of the business.

A **sole trader** is an organisation that is owned and run by one individual (the proprietor) and where there is no legal distinction between the owner and the business. The proprietor takes all profits and suffers all losses (subject to taxation). All the assets of the business are owned by the proprietor and all debts of the business are their debts and they must pay them from their personal resources. The proprietor has unlimited liability so that, if the business fails, they are personally liable for all its debts. It is a "sole" proprietorship in the sense that the proprietor has no partners.

A **partnership** is a method of trading which arises where a number of sole traders trade together. A partnership is defined in the Partnership Act 1890 as 'the relation which subsists between persons carrying on a business in common with a view of profit'. Most partnerships consist of between two and twenty partners although the large accountancy and legal partnerships have many more partners than this. Most partnerships also have unlimited liability.

A **private limited company** is a legal person that exists in its own right. This means that the company's finances are separate from the owners' personal finances. A company will therefore have shareholders – who may be individuals or other companies – who are generally not responsible for the debts of the business but may lose the money invested in the business if it were to fail. A private limited company must use the letters Ltd after its name and is not able to offer shares for sale to the general public.

A **public limited company** is an organisation that can offer shares for sale to the general public and its shares can be traded on the Stock Exchange. Such an organisation will use the letters Plc after its name. A public limited company must have at least two shareholders and must issue shares to the public of at least £50,000 before it can legally trade.

Different types of organisations have different rules regarding the preparation and publication of accounts.

A **franchise** is an organisation type where the success of one business is exploited by selling the company name and product to individuals wishing to invest in it by trading under the organisation's name. It is a method of obtaining rapid, often international, growth. Successful franchises include Subway and McDonalds. The franchisee will invest in the business, buying from the franchisor an almost pre-packaged business including the company name, suppliers, logo etc and will then operate the franchise paying a regular fee to the franchiser to cover the royalty of using the trademark name and an amount in respect of training and advisory services.

Task 1

What are the common aims and objectives of most types of organisation? Write down as many as you can before reviewing the suggested answers at the back of this workbook.

What are the differences in the aims and objectives between public and private sector organisations? Again, take some time to think about this and write down as many differences as you can before reviewing the answers.

How does the organisation type affect the behaviour of the organisation? Think about two very distinct organisation types to help you with this – perhaps a small local charitable trust and a large multinational plc.

The third sector

A third business sector exists which is made up of a group of organisations that are not strictly within either the public or the private sector. Organisations in this sector share common characteristics in that they:

- Are non-governmental
- Are value-driven
- Principally reinvest any financial surpluses to advance social, environmental or cultural objectives.

Examples include:

- Cooperatives
- Trusts
- Charities

Cooperatives are defined as 'An autonomous association of persons united voluntarily to meet their common economic, social and cultural needs and aspirations through a jointly owned and democratically controlled enterprise'. In short, a cooperative is an organisation owned and controlled equally by the people who use its services or who work in it. It is a legal entity which shares its earnings with its members as dividends and those members are often bound by common social or ethical principles. An example of a cooperative in the UK is The Cooperative Group.

www.co-operative.coop/aboutus/

Charities are organisations that take a distinct legal form and are run mainly by volunteers. To register as a charity with the Charity Commission, and thus obtain a special tax status, the charity must prove that it provides a benefit to the public. The law must recognise its aims, purposes and or objectives to be charitable and a number of rules and regulations must be obeyed to gain and then retain charitable status. Charities can also register as companies, in which case they must also comply with company law.

www.charity-commission.gov.uk

Organisations also differ from each other due to factors other than ownership and the organisation's aims and objectives.

Task 2

What other factors, apart from ownership and aims and objectives, affect an organisation?

Think about what makes one organisation different from another and list as many differences as you can. All these factors impact on how an organisation operates.

Review the suggested answers at the back of this workbook once you have done this.

ORGANISATION STRUCTURES

Many of the factors you will have listed as part of task 2 will affect the structure of an organisation. There are many different possible structures, and these are often affected by the size and age of the organisation. The structure of an organisation will affect how it operates and performs; an inappropriate structure can hinder the success of the organisation.

The structure of an organisation can be described as either flat or tall. A **flat** structure will not have many levels of management so the organisation chart would be quite flat, with each manager having many staff working for them (this is known as a wide span of control), and few management levels from the bottom of the organisation to the top. Organisations with flat structures can also have distinct operating divisions, perhaps with each having their own accounting functions. This type of organisation could also be said to be a decentralised organisation.

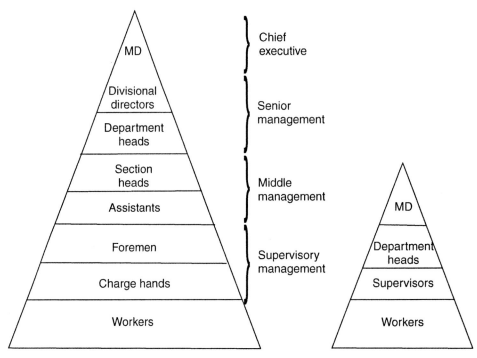

Tall and flat organisations

A **tall** organisation structure would be the opposite, with many levels of management and each manager would only be responsible for a small number of staff (a narrow span of control) A tall organisation can also be referred to as hierarchical – with many levels of hierarchy of management. A good example of an organisation with such a structure would be a government department, with many levels of managers and thousands of employees.

Often tall organisations are structured into pillars of expertise, so have centralised accounting functions (see chapter 3)

The trend in modern organisation structures is to flatten or delayer, removing tiers of management. No one structure is right or wrong, it must fit the organisation type and there are advantages and disadvantages of each. In your report analysing your chosen organisation you must be sure to ensure that you review whether the current organisation structure is appropriate for the type of organisation you are analysing, and whether any improvements can be recommended.

Task 3

What are the advantages of a tall organisation structure?
What are the advantages of a flat organisation structure?

Write down as many advantages as you can think of, reviewing again our explanations of these organisation types set out above. Review the suggested answers at the back of this workbook once you have done this.

Centralised organisations are those where the decision making power and authority are held at one central location, usually a Head Office function. Support functions such as the accounts department are also centralised, and will complete tasks for the whole organisation.

A **decentralised** organisation is one where the decision making power lies in each part of the business, perhaps within each division, factory, shop etc. In this type of organisation it is much harder to control the decisions made by staff, but easier to adapt to local markets and make innovative decisions regarding the organisation.

ORGANISATION STAKEHOLDERS

A stakeholder is anyone who is affected by the actions of the organisation. Stakeholders can be either internal or external to the organisation and directly or indirectly affected by its actions. There are many stakeholders common to most organisation types such as employees, customers, suppliers and owners but different organisations will also have stakeholders unique to them.

Task 4

List as many internal stakeholders to an organisation as you can.

List as many external stakeholders to an organisation as you can.

For each of the above consider what information needs the stakeholders may have, and how an organisation might meet these needs.

Try and break stakeholder groups down into subgroups with the same or similar information needs. For example do not just put employees as a stakeholder group. Different groups of employees may have differing information needs. Once complete review our suggested answers at the back of this workbook.

Stakeholders have important information needs and organisations must ensure that they communicate appropriately with them, though this may be through many different methods. The accounting systems of an organisation will have an important role in this and as part of your analysis and investigation into the accounting system you will be expected to consider how it meets the stakeholders' needs and what information it can provide.

Stakeholders also affect the ethics and culture of organisations. A good example of an organisation which has a large stakeholder group that may wield influence over its ethics and culture would be a football club such as Manchester United or Liverpool Football Club. A large stakeholder group, who as a whole take a deep interest in the actions of the organisation, would be the fans. An interesting argument would be how much power and influence they can wield over the organisation – think about how often fans influence decisions regarding the managers of the club or even, in the case of the two examples above, the owners.

Another example would be the John Lewis partnership which is owned and run by its employees. All permanent employees become partners of the organisation and share in its profits. This ownership has a clear impact on the aims, objectives and ethics and culture of the organisation.

These examples also highlight the need for good communication with large and/or powerful stakeholder groups.

THE REGULATORY FRAMEWORK OF ACCOUNTING

There are many regulations affecting how organisations operate, both within the accounting and wider business environment.

The way in which companies prepare their annual financial statements is regulated both by the law and the accounting profession. The purpose of this regulation is to try to ensure that the financial statements of different companies and different types of businesses are as comparable as possible.

Companies Act

The Companies Act 2006 sets out the way in which financial statements should be prepared and gives companies a detailed format of how the profit and loss account and balance sheet should be drawn up, the precise wording that should be used and a great deal of detail about the information that must be shown in the financial statements. For this unit you are expected to demonstrate a basic knowledge only of accounting regulations and how they impact on an organisation and therefore you will not be required to demonstrate a detailed knowledge of the Companies Act.

Accounting standards

As well as the legal regulation of companies' financial statements the accounting profession also regulates the preparation of financial statements by issuing accounting standards. The first UK accounting standards were produced around 40 years ago and were known as Statements of Standard Accounting Practice (SSAPs). The aim of the accounting standards is to reduce the variety of methods of dealing with accounting issues and to set out the best method to use in order to increase the comparability of the financial statements of different organisations.

A number of SSAPs are still in issue although the UK accounting framework is now under the control of the Accounting Standards Board which issues Financial Reporting Standards (FRSs) with the same aims as the old SSAPs. Companies must follow the requirements of SSAPs and FRSs when preparing financial statements but other non-corporate organisations have more flexibility. However, the SSAPs and FRSs do represent UK best accounting practice and are followed by sole traders and partnerships as well as companies not following International Standards (see below). UK accounting standards and UK company law (primarily the Companies Act we looked at earlier) are collectively known as UK Generally Accepted Accounting Practice (UK GAAP).

Accounting practice in the UK and elsewhere is increasingly influenced by **International Financial Reporting Standards (IFRSs)** and International Accounting Standards (IASs), issued by the International Accounting Standards Board (IASB).

Many companies are now preparing their financial statements under IFRSs which contain different terminology to that used in UK accounting standards. On 1 January 2012 the AAT moved from UK GAAP to IFRS terminology for its assessments.

For the purposes of this unit you are required to demonstrate knowledge that the accounting standards will **impact on the organisation** and the way in which it prepares its financial accounts (see chapter 3) and the influence they may have on controls (see chapter 5). We include both terminology used in IFRSs and UK GAAP. Usually, where the term differs for each, IFRSs terminology will be shown first (since this is the AAT's preferred terminology) with the UK GAAP terminology shown in brackets for information.

You will not be tested on the detail of particular accounting standards.

Other legislation

There are many other legislative regulations that impact on the organisation, either as a result of UK Acts of Parliament or European Directives. These include:

- Taxation regulations including VAT, Corporation tax and PAYE for employees

- Data protection law as set out in the Data Protection Act 1998

- Late payment law as set out in the Late Payment of Commercial Debt (Interest) Act 1998

- Health and Safety – The Health and Safety Executive are responsible in the UK for enforcing a variety of laws regarding safe and healthy work practices and places. www.hse.gov.uk

- Food Safety – The Food Standards Agency are responsible for enforcing a variety of regulations for all organisations that sell and handle food, from corner shops to restaurants. www.food.gov.uk

- Industry regulations – every industry has regulations that affect how it operates and, possibly, how it disposes of its waste. As part of your report you should include information regarding the regulations that affect your chosen organisation.

Accounting policies

Organisations also adopt their own accounting policies – rules as to how they construct their management and financial accounts. These are discussed in more detail in Chapter 3.

REPORT: INTRODUCTION TO THE ORGANISATION

To cover the outcomes of this chapter in your report you will need to write between one and two pages providing a brief outline of the organisation you have chosen to investigate and details of its current type and structure. You may find it appropriate to include an organisation chart in an appendix to help you explain the structure. Ensure you explain the ownership of the organisation and the key stakeholders affected by its actions.

Ensure that you clearly describe the aims and objectives of the organisation – to assist with this you may be able to research mission statements from its website or from published records and accounts.

You must also include a summary of the regulatory framework in which it operates, providing examples of both accounting and non-accounting regulations (if appropriate) with which it must comply.

Your report must be written in the third person only (that is no 'I' or 'we' or 'he' or 'she').

The report should be a series of short paragraphs showing each area of investigation. When you have completed it you should be able to map your work to the assessment criteria – see Chapter 7 on mapping your work to help you with this.

You must ensure that you include copies of any documents referred to in your report (for example an organisation chart showing the structure in place) in your appendices. This is important reference material for the person reading the final report.

Finally, if you feel that any of the relevant assessment criteria have not been covered specifically by this section, you should include technical notes in an appendix. Your assessor will be able to advise you whether this is required.

Checklist

- Write up your research of each area of investigation as outlined above

- Ensure you cover:
    - A brief background to the organisation
    - Its aims and objectives
    - External regulations affecting the organisation
    - External stakeholders

- Include copies of all relevant documents in the appendices

- Write only in the third person

- Use short, individually numbered paragraphs

- Map your work to the assessment criteria

Case Study Advice

When you have read the Case Study through you will notice most of the areas of the required research outlined above are clearly mentioned and some are implied. For example it may be helpful to construct an organisation chart from the information provided (to place in your appendices) to get a clear picture of the current organisation style and/or type.

You may also need to use your knowledge of common stakeholder groups in order to explain key stakeholders of the organisation and complete some research to understand the regulatory framework that might affect how it operates. Immerse yourself in the scenario and remember that the report must read in the same way as if it were your actual workplace. Use your skills, knowledge and imagination to supplement the case scenario if required.

The sample report at the back of this workbook will aid your understanding as to how to complete this. Remember to send your draft to your assessor for review – it will aid their authentication of your work and provide you with valuable feedback on your progress.

FAQS

1   **How much should I write in this section?** – This section should be between one and two pages in length and explain the organisation's ownership, structure, stakeholders (both internal and external) and the regulatory framework within which it operates. There is therefore a lot of competence to demonstrate so keep your work reasonably brief and do not write a history of the organisation, unless this helps explain it in the context of where it is today.

2   **What is an internal stakeholder?** – this is anyone who is affected by the actions of the organisation and is directly and internally linked to it. The term generally refers to employees, managers and supervisors for example. In the report you may split employees into different employee groups to enable you to better explain their relationship to the organisation.

3   **What is an external stakeholder?** – this is anyone who is affected by the actions of the organisation and is not internal to it. It can refer to many groups including customers, suppliers, the community, the government etc.

4   **How do I include external regulations?** – all organisations are bound by external regulations that affect how they operate. These include accounting and non-accounting regulations. Look at the industry that the organisation operates within and any regulations that may be specific to it. Talk to management within the organisation and also do some research on the internet. Include explanations of the regulations that affect the organisation.

5   **What appendices can I include for this section?** – The appendices to your report should be any documents that help explain the situation to the reader. Any diagrams should be included in the appendices and not in the body of the report. A good approach in this section would be to construct a simple organisation chart and include this to help explain how the organisation is structured.

6   **The AAT Case Study has limited information on this section, how do I supplement my writing?** – If you use what knowledge you have gained by working through this chapter you will see that general knowledge can supplement the Case Study. It may be that you can construct an organisation chart, from the information provided, and then conclude as to the structure of the organisation and whether the accounts department is centralised or decentralised. You can also use your knowledge, supplemented by careful reading of the scenario, to list the key stakeholders to the organisation, both internal and external, and to define their relationship to it.

chapter 3:
THE ACCOUNTS DEPARTMENT

chapter coverage 📖

In this chapter we will look at the accounts department as a function of an organisation and review different approaches to such functions in the context of structure.

The trend in organisations has been, over recent years, to centralise functions such as accounts and even to outsource all or some of the role of the accounts team to third parties. We will consider the impact that this has on the organisation and how it operates.

We will also review the role of the accounts department and the differences between management and financial accounts. Both have a different focus, approach and meet different stakeholder needs.

We will also briefly look at the management of the accounts department and how this impacts on its culture.

Following on from the theme of stakeholders, discussed in the previous chapter, we will look at key stakeholders to the accounts department and how the department might communicate with both internal and external stakeholder groups.

In this section of report you will therefore be expected to review and explain the structure and approach to the accounts department within your chosen organisation and review whether it is appropriate to it. After this review you will be expected to make suitable recommendations as to how the organisation of the accounts department might be improved.

LEARNING OUTCOMES

PIC 1.1 – Describe the purpose, structure and organisation of the accounting function and its relationship with other functions within the organisation.

PIC 1.2 – Explain the various business purposes for which the following accounting information is required:

- Income statement
- Forecast of statement of cash flows
- Statement of financial position

PIC 1.4 – Explain how the accounting systems are affected by the organisational structure, systems, procedures and business transactions

EAS 1.1 – Identify an organisation's accounting system requirements

THE ACCOUNTS DEPARTMENT

The preparation of accounts is a key function in any organisation, whether within the public or the private sector and includes many activities which can, in larger organisations, also be functions in their own right. These include:

- Accounts receivable (sales ledger)
- Accounts payable (purchase ledger)
- Payroll
- Costing
- Budgeting

The main aim of any accounting function is to accurately and fully process all accounting transactions for the organisation, whilst avoiding processing any invalid transactions, so that the information provided to stakeholders is correct and up to date.

How an organisation's accounting function is organised and structured depends on many of the factors discussed in chapter 2 including its size, age, ownership, stakeholders and objectives. These factors will also affect the specific tasks the function performs, for example the private sector will maintain detailed accounts for customers whereas the public sector will do so to a much lesser extent.

Organisations choose to keep functions such as accounting either centralised or decentralised and both approaches have their advantages and disadvantages.

Centralised functions

Centralisation is where an organisation chooses to place all staff who perform a particular function at the same location, regardless of where other activities are carried out. An example might be a large manufacturing organisation which chooses to have the accounts function sited at Head Office rather than in several different locations at the manufacturing sites.

Many organisations, such as Ford Motor Company, now choose to centralise such functions globally.

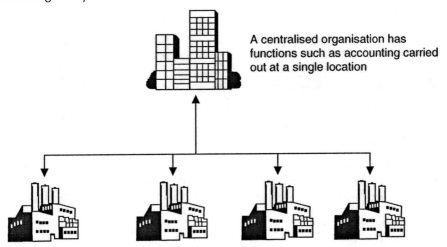

A centralised organisation has functions such as accounting carried out at a single location

Centralisation brings with it many advantages such as economies of scale as fewer staff overall are needed to complete the same amount of work. It may also bring disadvantages such as the creation of an 'Ivory Tower' function that is remote from the operational centres and has little or no involvement with the rest of the organisation.

Decentralisation

A decentralised approach to the accounting function would be where an organisation has chosen to have several separate accounts departments, perhaps one for each division or separate organisation entity such as factories. A decentralised approach often follows a structure and strategy where the organisation treats each of its parts as a separate profit making entity in its own right. Decentralisation may require more staff but can lead to better information flows and communication as the staff are based 'at site'. An example would be a manufacturing organisation with several factories, each with its own accounts team.

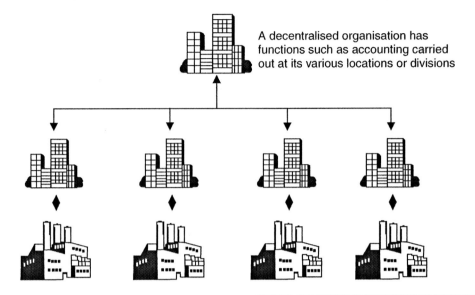

A decentralised organisation has functions such as accounting carried out at its various locations or divisions

---

Task 1

List as many advantages of having a centralised accounts function as you can.
What do you think are the disadvantages of such an approach?
What is your own organisation's approach – and do you think it is appropriate?

Review the suggested answers at the back of this workbook once you have completed this task.

Outsourcing

Many organisations take some, or more rarely all, of the functions carried out by an accounts department and not only centralise them but then choose to outsource this work to a third party, often under strict service level agreements (SLAs).

An example of a function that has seen an increase in outsourcing over recent years is payroll. Outsourcing is most popular for routine tasks, which are highly automated and rely on information technology for processing. As payroll skills and knowledge is also quite specialised it may be cheaper for small or medium sized organisations to 'buy in' the specialised knowledge from an organisation rather than employ staff with appropriate knowledge and experience. A payroll bureau will be able to share skilled staff across several organisations, producing economies of scale, and a cheaper service for customers.

THE ROLE OF THE ACCOUNTS DEPARTMENT

The role of the accounts department is primarily to provide information. Either internally through financial and management accounting information, or externally through financial accounting information in the form of published accounts.

Financial accounting

Financial accounting is the process of producing financial statements for decision makers, that provide the reader with an overview of the financial performance of the organisation. The decision makers concerned with the financial statements of an organisation might include many of the key internal and external stakeholders discussed in Chapter 2. This might include the owners, government agencies, banks and suppliers.

Financial accountants prepare financial accounting information for publication to people both internal and external to the organisation. They summarise financial data taken from the organisation's accounting records and publish it in the form of reports. The preparation of such reports is governed by company law and accounting standards, as discussed in Chapter 2.

Financial accounting includes the preparation of:

Income statement (Profit and loss account) - The INCOME STATEMENT of an organisation is a summary of the activity of the organisation during the year. It is, in simple terms:

INCOME minus EXPENSES equals PROFIT OR LOSS

If the income is greater than the expenses then a profit has been made. If the expenses exceed the income then a loss has been made.

However, despite the simple concept of the income statement it is normally laid out in a particular manner.

Income statement (profit and loss account)

	£	£
Revenue (sales)		44,000
Less: Cost of sales		
Opening inventory (stock)	2,400	
Purchases	28,000	
	30,400	
Less: Closing inventory (stock)	(3,200)	
Cost of sales		(27,200)
Gross profit		16,800
Less: Expenses		
Electricity	240	
Marketing	80	
Discount allowed	440	
Discount received	(280)	
Wages	10,400	
Travel	160	
Rent	600	
Telephone	320	
		(11,960)
Profit for the year (net profit)		4,840

The GROSS PROFIT is the profit earned by the trading activities of the business. As you can see it is calculated as revenue less the cost of those sales.

The second part of the income statement consists of a list of all of the EXPENSES of the business.

The PROFIT FOR THE YEAR (NET PROFIT) is the final profit of the business after all of the expenses have been deducted.

Statement of financial position (balance sheet) – Whereas the income statement (profit and loss account) is a history of the transactions of the business during the accounting period the STATEMENT OF FINANCIAL POSITION (BALANCE SHEET) is simply a 'snap shot' of the business on the final day of the accounting period.

The statement of financial position (balance sheet) is a list of all of the assets, liabilities and capital of the business. It is also an expression of the accounting equation. Remember that the accounting equation is:

ASSETS minus LIABILITIES equals CAPITAL

The statement of financial position (balance sheet) is a vertical form of the accounting equation. It lists and totals the assets of the business and deducts the liabilities. This total is then shown to be equal to the capital of the business.

Statement of financial position (balance sheet)

	£	£	£
Non-current (fixed) assets			10,200
Current assets:			
Inventory (stock)	3,200		
Receivables (debtors)	3,800		
Bank	800		
		7,800	
Current liabilities:			
Payables (creditors)		(2,400)	
Net current assets			5,400
			15,600
Long term liabilities:			
Loan			(2,000)
			13,600

Financed by:

	£
Opening capital	12,760
Add: profit	4,840
	17,600
Less: drawings	(4,000)
	13,600

The statement of financial position (balance sheet) falls naturally into two parts which are the two sides of the ACCOUNTING EQUATION – 'assets minus liabilities' and 'capital'.

The NON-CURRENT (FIXED) ASSETS are always shown as the first assets on the balance sheet being the major long-term assets of the business.

The CURRENT ASSETS of a business are its other shorter term assets. These are listed in particular order starting with the least liquid asset, inventory (stock), followed by receivables (debtors) and then finally the most liquid asset the bank account and then possibly followed by cash in hand or petty cash.

The CURRENT LIABILITIES of a business are the short term payables – the other title that is used for these in the UK is 'Creditors: amounts payable within one year'.

The NET CURRENT ASSETS figure is a sub-total of the current assets minus the current liabilities. The net current asset total is then added to the non-current asset total.

The LONG-TERM LIABILITIES are liabilities that are due to be paid after more than one year. In this case we have assumed that the loan is a long term loan, ie, repayable after more than one year. The total for long term liabilities is deducted from the total of non-current assets and net current assets to give the total shown on the statement of financial position. In terms of the accounting equation this is the total of the assets minus liabilities.

The CAPITAL section of the statement of financial position (balance sheet) shows the amounts that are owed to the owner of the business. This consists of the amount of capital owed to the owner at the start of the accounting period plus the profit that the business has earned (this figure of £4,840 is the profit taken from the income statement) less the drawings that the owner has taken out of the business during the accounting period. The total of the capital section will, of course, equal the total of the assets minus the liabilities.

Note that drawings are part of the statement of financial position (balance sheet) and are not included as expenses – they are a reduction of the amount that is owed to the owner by the business.

Income and expenditure accounts

Sole traders, partnerships and companies all produce an income statement (profit and loss account) and a statement of financial position (balance sheet) Other types of not-for-profit organisations such as clubs and societies do not prepare an income statement showing a 'profit' as their aim is not necessarily to make a profit. However these organisations do produce something very similar known as an income and expenditure account which shows a 'surplus' if income exceeds expenditure. An example of an income and expenditure account together with its associated statement of financial position (balance sheet) are shown below for illustration.

Income and expenditure account for Crowfield Rugby Club for the year ended 31 December 20X0

	£	£
Income:		
Subscription income		7,170
Bar profit		3,100
Dinner dance profit		400
		10,670
Less: Expenditure		
Loss on sale of grass cutter	100	
Depreciation of grass cutter	250	
Rent and rates	1,300	
Electricity	2,040	
Groundsman's expenses	700	
Club secretary's expenses	900	
Fixtures fees	3,500	
Sundry expenses	200	
		(8,990)
Surplus of income over expenditure		1,680

Statement of financial position (balance sheet) as at 31 December 20X0

	£	£
Non-current assets at cost		1,000
Less: provision for depreciation		(250)
Net book value		750
Bar inventory	1,800	
Subscriptions in arrears	30	
Prepayment	300	
Bank	1,550	
		3,680
		4,430
Less: Payables		
Subscriptions in advance	120	
Accruals	240	
		(360)
		4,070

	£
Accumulated fund at 1 January 20X0	2,390
Surplus of income over expenditure	1,680
Accumulated fund at 31 December 20X0	4,070

Manufacturing accounts

A further type of accounting statement that some manufacturing organisations will produce is a manufacturing account. This is a structured list of all of the expenses incurred in the production process culminating in the total cost of the goods manufactured in the period. An example of a manufacturing account is given below for illustration.

Manufacturing account for the year ended 31 March 20X1

	£	£
Opening inventory (stock) of raw materials		6,000
Purchases of raw materials		70,000
		76,000
Less: closing inventory (stock) of raw materials		(8,000)
Direct materials used		68,000
Direct labour		36,000
Direct expenses		1,900
Prime cost		105,900
Production overheads:		
Supervisor's salary	17,000	
Factory rent	8,000	
Machinery depreciation	6,000	
Factory light and heat	4,000	
		35,000
		140,900
Add: opening work in progress		4,000
		144,900
Less: closing work in progress		(4,900)
Manufacturing cost of goods completed		140,000

Accounting policies

When final accounts are being prepared for an organisation they will be prepared according to company law, accounting standards and the organisation's own accounting policies. The organisation's accounting policies govern the precise way in which the rules set out in the accounting standards are applied to the organisation's particular circumstances.

For example, organisations are generally required to depreciate their non-current assets. However, the precise rate at which depreciation is applied is determined by the management of the organisation in the form of an accounting policy.

The choice of accounting policies that an organisation makes is fundamental to the picture shown by the final accounts and therefore an International Accounting Standard (IAS) has been issued on this area – IAS 8 *Accounting policies, changes in accounting estimates and errors*. (UK accounting standard FRS 18 *Accounting policies* also covers this area). You do not require detailed knowledge of IAS 8 (or FRS 18) for this unit.

Management accounting

Management accounting differs from financial accounting in that it is internally focused and is less bound by strict rules and reporting standards and more by the needs of the organisation's management.

Management accounting aims to provide management with financial information that they can use in order to make critical decisions that affect how the organisation is run. Management accountants prepare information solely for the use of internal stakeholders. This includes the preparation of information such as:

- Budgets
- Costing
- Standard costs
- Variance reports
- Ratio analysis
- Sales figures for products and or divisions
- Inventory levels
- Profitability reports
- Any other internal information prepared using financial data

All of the above management accounting reports would be used internally, within the organisation, by management to help them manage the organisation's profitability and cash flow. They will be used to make decisions on resourcing and may form part of performance management appraisal. For example, a stores manager might be set the objective to keep inventories to an acceptable level, especially in an organisation such as Bayou Stores Limited as per the sample Case Study at the back of this workbook, where some of these inventories include food products.

Task 2

Research what internal management accounting reports are prepared within your own organisation.

What value to do they have? Think about how managers might use them to make decisions about the organisation.

What additional information might management need to make better, more informed decisions?

MANAGEMENT OF THE ACCOUNTS DEPARTMENT

How a department is managed has a large impact on the culture within it. In this context, culture can be regarded as 'The way we do things around here' and may be very different from the way an organisation might want it to be.

Management affect the culture within the organisation because they set the standard for how the organisation operates on a day to day basis. This is often what makes one organisation different from another. The culture within an organisation may be one of team work – where everyone helps each other to ensure all tasks are completed on time and appropriately by the team as a whole, or one of each member of staff keeping to their own roles and responsibilities. There may be a culture of control, where all rules and procedures are adhered to at all times, or one that is more relaxed where controls are more informal and trust is an important part of the controls in place.

One way to illustrate this is to consider how a new driver might have to drive to pass their driving test, with the examiner sat next to them in the car, and then to consider how they may drive 15 years later. Both would be safe, and keeping within certain rules, but the driving itself might be quite different!

No one culture is right or wrong and different styles of management will be appropriate for different types of organisation.

Management styles

The style of management in organisations directly affects how the organisation operates, and therefore its culture. The main styles of management are:

Democratic – a democratic manager delegates authority to his or her staff. The manager gives them complete responsibility to complete tasks using their own work methods, but within certain organisation boundaries. This is also known as empowerment of staff. A democratic manager will also involve employees in decision making and this can be motivating. It can however lead to slower decision making as all staff are consulted first.

Autocratic – an autocratic manager will dictate orders to staff and make all decisions without consultation with them. Therefore decision making is quick, but staff are not consulted which can de-motivate them. They are not empowered and can feel undervalued.

Consultative – a consultative manager is one with a combination of the democratic and autocratic management styles. Views and opinions will be asked for from staff before decisions are made but the ultimate decision making still lies with the manager.

Laissez faire – a laissez faire manager will set their staff a task and then give them complete freedom to complete it in any way they like. The manager will be there to answer questions and to perhaps counsel and coach staff to complete the work, but will not be involved in actually doing it. Staff can be motivated by this but can also feel that they lack guidance and do not reach the goals set.

It should be noted that no one management style is right or wrong. Which style is right for an organisation depends on the factors below and on the subordinate styles of the staff working within the organisation.

Other factors affecting culture

Culture will depend on many factors, not just management style. In this unit you will need to briefly consider the management style and culture in place in your chosen organisation and whether it is appropriate to it. In doing this you will have to think carefully about the organisation and the factors that influence the culture within the accounts department, and whether it is appropriate to the organisation or not.

Factors affecting an organisations culture might include:

History of the organisation

Ownership

Aims and objectives

Industry the organisation is in

Structure

Management

Rules and procedures

Customer expectations

Technology

Size

Stakeholders to the accounts department

There are many internal stakeholders in an organisation that may be reliant on the information the accounts department produces, in order that they can carry out their own function for the organisation both effectively and efficiently.

Task 3

Read through the sample Case Study at the back of this workbook. This is the Case Study published by the AAT as an example of what you will be provided with if you are unable to complete this unit based on your own organisation.

The Case Study provides you with information on a fictitious organisation. In order to write your final report you will need to imagine you work for that organisation, that the scenario is real, and consists of the knowledge you have built up by working there.

Who are the stakeholders in the accounts department of Bayou Stores Limited and what are their information needs – both financial and management?

Think of stakeholders that may be mentioned specifically by the scenario and also general ones that would exist within any typical organisation.

Are there any information needs that are not currently being met? What additional information could be produced to ensure decision makers are better informed?

REPORT

When completing this section of your report you will need to research the information your organisation's accounts department produces, both for external and internal use. You will also need to research how your accounts department is organised and structured and perhaps include an organisation chart in an appendix.

As part of your accounts department section you should briefly explain where the accounting department of the organisation is based and whether it is centralised, decentralised or outsourced. You should also include how the accounts department communicates with other parts of the organisation.

You will need to review whether financial and management reports are adequate and whether information needs of decision makers are being adequately met. You could do this by completing an analysis of internal stakeholders to the accounts department and reviewing their information needs. From this review you will be expected to make recommendations as to how to improve the organisation's accounting systems. Chapter 4 contains more advice on how to complete this.

Checklist

- Review the organisation's accounts department structure and how it communicates with other parts of the organisation.
- Review the internal stakeholders to the accounts department.
- Review what financial and management accounting reports are being produced.
- Review whether information needs are being met.
- Research critical incidents that may have occurred because information needs have not been met.
- Include diagrams such as organisation charts of the accounts department in the appendices.
- Write short, individually numbered paragraphs
- Write only in the third person.
- Make recommendations to improve information needs not currently being met (you may put this in a separate recommendations section if you wish).

Case Study Advice

When you have read the Case Study through you will notice some areas of the required research outlined above are clearly mentioned and some are not. Consider the Case Study to be a story about an organisation, so areas not covered perhaps do not feature in the organisation at present. For example you may need to construct an organisation chart of the accounts team in order that you can fully analyse its structure and complete a review of critical incidents so that you can review whether information needs are met.

You may also need to assume whether basic financial and management reports are being produced and whether they are being used by key decision makers. In the sample report in the back of this workbook we have assumed that not many reports are currently being produced by the accounts team. This is because the system is decentralised and there does not appear to be evidence that the decision makers are using them. The owner, John Bayou, was unaware of the size of the overdraft for example.

Immerse yourself in the scenario and remember that the report must read in the same way as if it were your actual workplace. Use your skills, knowledge and imagination to supplement the case scenario and to make a detailed analysis of the situation, and to make recommendations to improve, clearly explaining the benefit to the organisation.

The sample report at the back of this workbook will aid your understanding as to how to complete this. Remember to send your draft to your assessor for review – it will aid their authentication of your work and provide you with valuable feedback on your progress.

FAQS

1   **How do I research the structure of my accounts department?** - You should look at the documentation your organisation produces, often found on organisation intranets, or interview your accounts managers and draw up an organisation chart yourself. This will help you understand the current structure of the department, and whether it meets the organisation's needs.

2   **I work in a large organisation with several large sections to the accounts department, how do I include this in my report?** – Within your report you can include brief detail explaining the overall size and structure of your accounts department, and how the organisation ensures it does (or does not!) communicate with other parts of the business. You will see in Chapter 4 that as you start the detailed research on the weaknesses within the accounts system that you can then focus this research on just one part of the system, rather than the department as a whole.

3   **Where do I include the results of this research in my report?** – This chapter can be included as one section in your report – the accounts department. It can include basic, brief, information about the accounts department and its stakeholders. It will also include a brief description as to how the accounts system is structured. This is to set the scene for the reader so that they better understand the context of the main review completed in the next section. In the internal stakeholder analysis you can include detail of information needs not met, based around your research of the system and the information it produces plus critical incidents that have occurred. There will be more guidance on how to do this in Chapter 4 so it may be helpful to work through that chapter first.

4   **How do I review critical incidents in my workplace to understand if information needs have been met?** – A good place to start would be to interview management and staff who work as part of the accounts team. Also to review any recent reports such as internal audit reports on the work of the department or team. Remember that the reason you are completing this research is to understand where information needs are not being met. As part of your interviews you could include this question for key decision makers to see what information they would like that they are currently not receiving.

5   **My organisation/manager is concerned about the confidentiality of what I put in my report** – First of all you should note that this report is looking at the organisation, its accounting systems and information and making recommendations to improve them. This should benefit the organisation. You are putting this information into a professional management report and submitting it to your assessor for assessment. The work is confidential and your assessor will not be reproducing it or sharing it with other students. To complete this report you do not need to share critical or sensitive information and your assessor will be able to advise you if management have concerns about certain aspects of your report. You must accept though that at the end of the report your assessor will require a statement, from you manager and on company headed paper, that the work is your own, unaided and a true reflection of the organisation. If your manager or supervisor is unwilling to provide this then you must not complete the work on your workplace, but on an AAT Case Study instead.

6   **What Financial and Management Accounting Reports do I need to include in my research?** – Try and research as many reports as necessary that are produced by the accounts department. You are not required to complete a detailed report on each, or even include them all in the appendices. You should ensure that you at least cover the income statement (profit and loss account), the forecast of statement of cash flows (cash flow statement) and statement of financial position (balance sheet). Try and cover both financial accounting reports and management accounting reports.

chapter 4:
ACCOUNTING SYSTEMS

---

chapter coverage 📖

In this chapter we will look at some examples of how accounting systems might be structured and consider how they provide information to key stakeholders of the organisation.

We will then consider how to assess whether the accounting systems in place are suitable for the organisation and whether any improvements could be made to them.

Following on from that we will introduce the importance of controls within accounting departments and systems. We will look at the role controls play and consider examples of basic controls that should be in place. Within this section we will look at the importance of procedures and documentation, as a control tool, but also as a support to the individuals who use the accounting systems.

An example of documentation we will consider in more detail is the mapping of accounting systems and workflow. This can be completed by constructing diagrams such as flowcharts and we will look at the value and purpose of these.

We will then consider how to identify weaknesses in accounting systems – looking at tools to assist us with this such as a SWOT and / or PEST analysis. We will then consider recommendations to improve the systems and address weaknesses identified.

Finally we will explain how to write up this part of the report and include tips for those using a Case Study scenario.

LEARNING OUTCOMES

PIC 1.4 – Explain how the accounting systems are affected by the organisational structure, systems, procedures and business transactions

PIC 3.1 – Identify weaknesses in accounting systems:

- Potential for errors
- Exposure to possible fraud

PIC 3.2 – Explain how an accounting system can support internal control

PIC 3.3 – Identify ways of supporting individuals who operate accounting systems using:

- Training
- Manuals
- Written information
- Help Menus

PIC 3.4 – Explain the value and benefit to a specific organisation of different types of accounting systems and software packages.

EAS 1.2 – Review record keeping systems to confirm whether they meet the organisation's requirements for financial information

EAS 1.3 – Identify weaknesses in and the potential for improvements to, the accounting system and consider their impact on the operation of the organisation

EAS 1.5 – Review methods of operating for cost effectiveness, reliability and speed.

EAS 2.2 – Identify the effects that any recommended changes would have on the users of the system

EAS 2.3 – Enable individuals who operate accounting systems to understand how to use the system to fulfil their responsibilities

ACCOUNTING SYSTEMS

A system is any function that takes an input, processes it, and then produces an output. An ACCOUNTING SYSTEM is a system that takes raw data as its input, processes this, and then produces many outputs as discussed in Chapter 3.

The aim of any accounting system is to fully support the accounting team to process accurately and fully all accounting transactions so that financial and management information provided to stakeholders is accurate and complete.

If an accounting system within an organisation is not effective in completing this objective then the accounting information may be incorrect and not available to stakeholders when key decisions need to be made.

There are many different types of computerised accounting systems that exist within organisations and for this section of your report you are not expected to know particular computer packages but instead to understand that an accounting system consists of many different inputs, processes and outputs and that systems can be both computerised and manual. Either or both may be appropriate to your organisation and to complete this section of your report you will be expected to analyse your chosen system, map its processes, analyse its strengths and weaknesses and then make recommendations to improve it.

Accounting systems within organisations can be centralised or decentralised. The definitions of these are very similar to those for the department itself as discussed in Chapter 3. A **centralised** accounting system is one where all the data is stored at a central location, and accounts staff process it centrally, although this may be by accessing the system from many different locations.

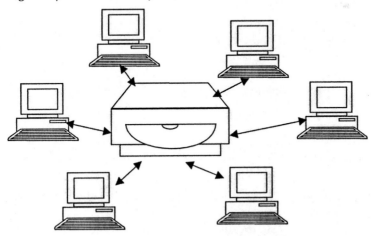

A centralised accounting system

A **decentralised** system is one where the data is stored and processed separately, perhaps independently by staff at different locations or with different computers.

There is no link between processes, each being formed independently of each other.

Task 1

What are the advantages of a centralised system?

What advantages would a decentralised system have?

Which do you think would be more appropriate to Bayou Stores Ltd as featured in the example Case Study at the back of this workbook?

List out the advantages of both types of system and then read back through the Case Study and think about what type of system is more appropriate to Bayou and why. Consider what information the key stakeholders in Bayou need and whether these information needs are met by the current system. Review our suggested answers at the back of this workbook when you have completed this task.

Examples of accounting systems

As already mentioned, a system is any activity that takes an input and processes it into an output. This can be computerised or manual. Examples of systems within an accounts department might be:

- The processing of payroll
- Recording income
- Recording purchases
- Paying suppliers
- Calculating standard costs
- Recording and banking receipts from customers
- Recording and managing petty cash
- Recording of time worked on clients / jobs
- Receipt and payment of expenses

All of the above would be suitable accounting systems for you to analyse in detail within your organisation for the completion of your report.

You are required by the learning outcomes to include a review of how the accounting systems in your organisation are structured, and whether they are appropriate to it and then to complete a more detailed analysis of one part of the system in particular, mapping how it currently operates and analysing any strengths and/or weaknesses within it. From this you are then expected to make recommendations to improve the accounting system.

The system you choose to analyse in detail can be your own role at work or the work of your department of team. It could also be one part of your role –

especially if you work in a small team where you each take on several processes or functions.

For example, you could investigate the purchase ledger function in your organisation, or the credit control or payroll function.

Whichever you choose it should be of sufficient value to the organisation (petty cash or expenses would not be sufficient unless they account for a large amount of expenditure in the organisation and take up a significant amount of the time of the accounting team).

The system you choose should ideally also be analysed with reference to appropriate controls, which will be a later section in your report.

If you are unsure as to what to do you should discuss this with your assessor and include your approach in your project proposal to ensure you receive appropriate feedback and support.

It may be helpful when doing this to consider yourself to be a consultant in the work place.

SYSTEM CONTROLS

All of the systems in place, in any department of any organisation, must be controlled in order that they operate safely, efficiently and effectively. Controls can include computerised controls (such as passwords or restrictions on staff performing certain operations) or manual (such as internal audit reviews and supervisory checks).

Accounting systems often have controls built into them to ensure they meet certain regulations and or requirements and then have formal reviews of these controls by auditors and or management to ensure they are appropriate and effective.

Internal controls are discussed in more detail in Chapter 5 where we look at specific examples of controls and the role of the internal auditing team. For this section we will address the importance of controls within accounting systems in general.

Controls are required because systems need to adapt and change, as the internal and/or external environment changes. They also ensure that the system continues to operate safely. In the concept of accounting systems they therefore ensure that the system is keeping within the regulatory framework and the rules and procedures of the organisation.

Specific controls will be discussed in more detail in the next chapter but for now we will consider one control in particular – that of documenting the accounting system including the procedures and/or user manuals for those that operate it.

Task 2

What are the advantages of an accounts department having a full user manual for all activities that take place within it?

What might the disadvantages of such an approach be?

Write down as many advantages and disadvantages as you can before reviewing the suggested answers.

Producing adequate documentation to map an accounting system, and provide manuals to assist users, is an intensive process, and such documents can quickly become out of date if the system is subject to change. It will, however, ensure that the way in which the system is required to operate is set out for users and will assist them in making sure the information output from the system is on time and of the correct quality.

Other important controls to consider within the accounting system itself are passwords and access controls. Accounting systems are complex and in any size of organisation it can be possible to restrict access to the system so that only staff that need access to particular functions are provided with it.

This can be completed in two ways. Firstly a system of passwords can be set up so that different parts of the system require different passwords to access. Staff can then only be provided with access to the parts of the system required.

Systems also often have administrator access where nominated administrators can set up access, but only to specific sections of the system. For example so that a accounts payable (purchase ledger) clerk cannot access the accounts receivable (sales ledger) or payroll functions. These are important controls so that staff can not complete operations that are not related to their role. It also aids the division of responsibilities so that certain key staff can not perform all the activities necessary to carry out fraud.

For example, if a accounts payable clerk is able to raise a purchase order, book goods into inventory and then process an invoice, they may be able to purchase goods for their own use, and then process the payment through the organisation's system. By not allowing the same member of staff access to all three of these activities the risk of fraud is significantly reduced.

When passwords are used by staff there should also be controls set in place regarding their use and control.

Task 3

Imagine you are the manager of an accounts department and are in the process of implementing a new accounting system.

All staff are being provided with their own passwords to access the parts of the system necessary to perform their work.

What rules would you put in place regarding the use and controls of passwords? Why are these important?

You will find this task easier if you think about the possible consequences of poor controls on passwords. Review the suggested answer once you have done so.

ANALYSING SYSTEMS

System flowchart

As already mentioned, all processes consist of a series of inputs that are processed into outputs. In a payroll process the input will be the staff hours worked, pay scales etc. The process would be to calculate the payroll and the output would be that the staff are paid. Each stage of this process can be analysed in detail and it may be helpful to **draw a system flowchart**. This shows the key decision making processes, inputs and outputs and can be included in the appendices to your report.

There are many ways of drawing a flowchart with symbols to show each stage of the process. Although these methods are appropriate, and can be used if you have studied them in the past, a simple flow chart can also be used that clearly shows the flow of the system using boxes and text.

For example:

Reading through the sample Case Study on Bayou Stores Limited at the back of this workbook it is relatively straightforward to complete a simple system flowchart of the payroll system. An appropriate one could be:

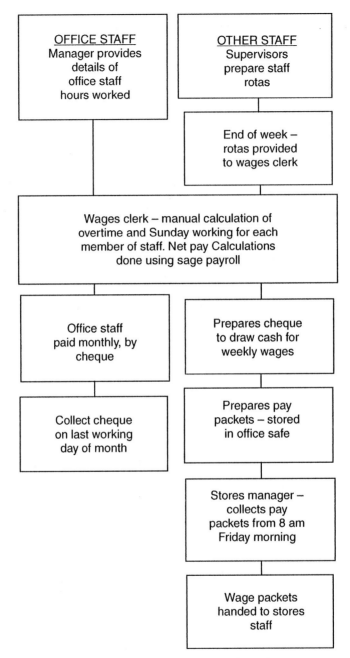

The above flowchart reflects our interpretation of the information provided in the Case Study scenario. When completing a system flowchart your are aiming to map out the system process as accurately as possible. If you are working from a case study then you may find that not all the information required is available. For example, the flowchart set out above assumes that the manager must provide details of office staff working hours. This is not explicit in the scenario itself.

By completing a system flowchart and mapping a process in detail, you should start to identify some improvements which can be made to the system and to the organisation. It is a requirement of this unit that appropriate recommendations be made to improve your selected system.

Task 4

Complete a system flowchart for the accounts payable function using the sample Case Study information at the back of this workbook.

Having completed this, and also by reviewing the example flowchart for the payroll process – what recommendations can you think of to improve these systems for the organisation?

SWOT analysis

Another tool to aid you to analyse the system in detail is a SWOT analysis. SWOT stands for:

Strengths
Weaknesses
Opportunities
Threats

The **Strengths** and **Weaknesses** to a system will be internal factors that either make it particularly effective or demonstrate clear weaknesses within it.

An example strength may be that a payroll system is operated by knowledgeable and experienced staff and a weakness might be that is a manual process, dependent on manual calculation which presents many opportunities for human error.

Once strengths and weaknesses have been identified then recommendations can be considered to address the weaknesses.

Opportunities and **Threats** are external to the actual system itself. It may be an opportunity to train more staff in payroll qualifications and a threat that information and legislation relating to payroll is subject to frequent change (tax codes, tax rates, NI contributions etc).

It is sometimes harder to identify external factors such as these but you should try and consider as many as you can – they will also help you to identify recommendations to improve the system.

Task 5

Read through the sample Case Study provided at the back of this workbook. Complete a SWOT analysis as below, focusing on the strengths and weaknesses of the internal accounting systems, and the opportunities and threats on the organisation as a whole.

Strengths

Weaknesses

Opportunities

Threats

Once you have completed this, review our suggested answers. Did you come up with similar Strengths, Weaknesses, Opportunities and Threats? Sometimes answers can be down to interpretation, especially between Strengths and Opportunities and Weaknesses and Threats. Do not worry about which heading you listed each under, it is enough that you identified them.

In the section of your report that completes the analysis of an accounting system you should write a summary of a SWOT analysis focusing on the weaknesses identified in the system. The SWOT analysis itself should be placed in the report's appendices, with reference to it within the summary.

PEST analysis

A final tool that may assist you in analysing your chosen system is a PEST analysis. A PEST analysis investigates four factors that may affect your organisation and the system. These four factors are:

Political
Economic
Social
Technological

Political factors – There are a variety of political factors that can affect the operation of an accounting system. These might include the following:

- Changes in NIC rates
- Changes in VAT rates
- Changes in company legislation regarding publication of financial statements
- Changes in financial reporting standards

Economic factors – Examples of economic factors that might affect the accounting system are:

- Increase/decrease in the volume of transactions due to general or specific changes in the economy and customer demands
- Changes in the availability and wage rate of the labour force
- The staff available to work in the accounting function
- The budget applied to the accounting function

General or specific economic changes may lead to an increase or decrease in the general level of transactions of an organisation. This will have a direct effect on the number of transactions within an accounting function although not necessarily on the nature of those transactions or the method of operations.

Social factors – Social factors that might affect the accounting system could include the following:

- Changing work patterns such as flexitime and home working
- Family commitments leading to changes such as part time working and job sharing
- Employment legislation

Technological factors – Examples of technological factors that might cause changes in the accounts system might be:

- Advances in computer technology
- Security issues
- Technological fraud
- On-line banking

In the section of your report that contains the analysis of an accounting system write a summary of a PEST analysis and make reference to it in the appendices.

You should now have completed enough research into the chosen accounting system to be able to make some recommendations for improvement.

Remember that your recommendations do not have to be implemented – the purpose of your report is to investigate and analyse and then to make recommendations to improve – not to have these recommendations put into place.

The **learning outcomes** for this unit requires you to make your recommendations clear, in an easily understood format and to support them with a clear rationale as to why you have concluded that they are appropriate. In order to demonstrate competence in this area you are required to fully justify *all* your recommendations, not just those relating to this section, plus explain them in summary format in an Executive Summary (more on this in chapter 7).

REPORT

When completing this section of your report you will firstly need to decide which part of the accounting system you are going to review, and make recommendations to improve. Depending on the size of your organisation you may choose to analyse the whole system, or just one part of it. Your assessor should be able to advise you on this. You will then need to conduct a complete review of the part of the accounting system you have chosen.

An effective way to start this would be to first complete a SWOT analysis. The SWOT analysis itself would be included as one of the appendices of the report. You would then summarise the outcomes of this in the report itself.

The AAT suggest that in order to do this you break this section of your report into several smaller sections:

- Working methods and practices
- Record keeping systems
- Training
- Fraud
- Internal systems and control

The next chapters contain more detail on both internal control systems and fraud and after you have studied them you may add to your SWOT analysis. We have also only included three of the above areas in this section of our sample report at the back of this workbook; working methods and practices, record keeping systems and training. We have kept Fraud and Internal Controls for a separate report section. This breaks up this section and makes it more manageable to write and review.

Once you have completed the SWOT analysis you may then wish to complete a separate PEST analysis. Again, you would put the actual PEST analysis in the appendices and include a summary of the results in the report. In both cases you must make reference to the appendices in the main body of the report.

You should at this point have identified detailed weaknesses within the system and be able to write up recommendations to improve them. This can be a separate sub section or a separate section of your report entirely. There must be a recommendation for each of the weaknesses you have identified, and they should appear in the same order as the weaknesses. This makes your final report easier to read and more logical. The recommendations should be in sufficient detail so as to clearly explain why they should be implemented, and the benefit to the organisation that would result.

It may be that one recommendation would cover several of the weaknesses, if this is the case the recommendation does not need to be repeated but it should be clear as to which of the weaknesses it covers.

At this point you should not detail the costs and benefits to the organisation of your recommendations, other than brief reasons as to why they should be implemented. The costs and benefits will be included in a later section.

Checklist

- Decide which part of the accounting system you will analyse, ensure you discuss this with your assessor

- Complete a SWOT analysis on your chosen system or part of a system

- Put the SWOT analysis in the appendices

- Write a summary in the main report

- Refer to the appendices

- Complete a PEST analysis, if appropriate, on your chosen system or part of a system. Ensure it is in the appendices, with reference to it in the main report

- Write a sub-section / main section on recommendations to improve the system, ensuring each weakness you have identified is addressed in turn

- Ensure all recommendations are fully explained in relation to the benefit they will bring to the organisation

- Write short, individually numbered paragraphs

- Write only in the third person

Case Study Advice

The Case Study contains a lot of information about the whole accounting function in the organisation and you are not expected to write this section of your report on all of it.

Instead, read it through carefully and decide on one section of the system (perhaps payroll or accounts payable (purchase ledger)) to analyse. Ideally you will also investigate this part of the system when looking into internal controls and fraud risk. Perhaps pick the system in respect of which you have the most practical experience or the one that appears to have the most room for improvement.

If in doubt, discuss this with your assessor and remember that if the detail contained within the case scenario is weak then you can supplement it with your own research or knowledge of the work place. Also remember to ensure that the report reads as if you work in the organisation and are making the recommendations to your own manager.

FAQS

1   **I am not sure which part of the accounting system to investigate – which should I choose?** – This depends on your particular organisation and accounting system. The system you choose to investigate should not be so large that it will take you months of research and take pages to document and not so small that it is not sufficient in importance in your organisation. A good guide would be to consider the size of your organisation and the number of staff working on the various systems and processes. Anything that takes up a small amount of one member of staff's time is probably too small. Any system that takes several staff to operate could be too large. If in doubt discuss this with your assessor.

2   **I want to investigate more than one system – is this OK?** – This is dependent on the size of the system(s) and the amount of work involved. Remember that the overall finished report should be approximately 4,000 words (excluding the appendices) and that you do not want to spend too long on this section of your report as you have other key sections to complete. If your organisation has requested that you investigate several areas and this is going to add practical value to your finished report then discuss this with your assessor.

3   **I am investigating the system in this section: how do I keep this separate from my review of internal controls and fraud?** – The analysis of the accounting system section also includes sub-sections on internal controls and fraud. You will see in Chapter 6 that you are required to complete a Fraud Matrix as part of this work, and therefore to specifically address the potential for fraud within the system. As you complete your SWOT analysis though you will automatically consider weaknesses within the controls in place. If the weaknesses relate specifically to internal controls and/or fraud then put them under these headings in your report. If the weaknesses are more general then address them under other appropriate headings. It is more important to ensure the weaknesses are included, and recommendations made to address them, than their precise position in the analysis.

4   **Should I draw a system flow chart?** – A detailed flow chart is required. Your aim is to map the processes and flow of the system so that the reader of your report can gain an understanding of how the system works.

5   **Why should I put the flow chart, SWOT and PEST analysis in the appendices rather than the main report?** – A professional document such as this should not include any tables, charts or diagrams in the main body of the report. These are kept to the appendices to be referred to when required. This will also help to keep your word count down!

6   **I am struggling to think of opportunities and threats in respect of my system, what can I do?** – You could address this section by asking your supervisor or manager to suggest some. Another idea is to conduct a little research into the overall environment in which the organisation operates. If after these two possibilities you are still finding this difficult then do not worry as including the strengths and weaknesses are far more important.

7   **Any recommendations I come up with are never going to be implemented by my organisation so what should I do?** – This does not matter. The outcome of this unit should be a professional management report making recommendations to improve the organisation. They do not have to be implemented and while it is hoped that they would at least be reviewed and considered by management this does not actually have to happen.

8   **My organisation has really efficient and effective systems in place – so there will be no recommendations to improve** – This is fine as long as you can demonstrate to your assessor that you have fully researched all of the areas of investigation and from that research you have concluded that there are no improvements to be made. It would be rare for a report to contain no recommendations at all.

chapter 5:
INTERNAL CONTROLS

---

chapter coverage 📖

In this chapter we will define internal control, providing examples that relate to both the meeting of organisational requirements and statutory ones. We will provide examples of control activities for three key accounting functions – sales, purchases and payroll.

We will then review the aims and objectives of internal audit within an organisation, or the need for similar activities in an organisation that is perhaps too small to have an internal audit department.

We will look at the assessment of control risk and how it might assess the integrity of any controls in place.

We will then cover how to include internal controls within the analysis of the accounting system section of your report, perhaps adding to the SWOT analysis already prepared as part of Chapter 4.

Finally we will include tips for those writing their report from the AAT Case Study scenario.

LEARNING OUTCOMES

PIC 2.3 – Explain methods that can be used to detect fraud within an accounting system

PIC 2.4 – Explain the types of controls that can be put in place to ensure compliance with statutory or organisational requirements

PIC 3.2 – Explain how an accounting system can support internal control

---

INTERNAL CONTROL

Organisations need good, robust internal control systems in order to reduce the risk of fraud and ensure that accounting systems operate appropriately and change as the environment around them changes.

Internal controls are barriers in place within an organisation to protect it from fraudulent activities and human error and to ensure that it complies with applicable laws and regulation. They ensure that the organisation is working to meet its aims and objectives.

An example of an internal control is segregation of duties where the same member of staff does not open the post, record cheques received and also bank them. More examples are provided later in this chapter.

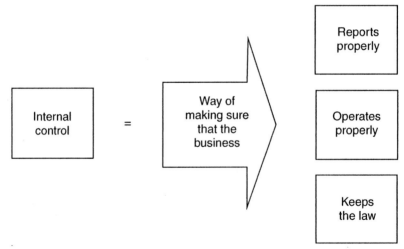

A system of internal control includes procedures and processes designed and implemented to address the risk that the aims and objectives of an organisation will not be met.

A system of internal control consists of the following elements.

- The control environment
- The risk assessment process
- The information system – covered by chapter 4
- Control activities
- Monitoring of controls

Control environment

The CONTROL ENVIRONMENT is formed by the attitudes, awareness and actions of management and those responsible for ensuring that the internal controls within an organisation meet that organisation's needs.

In other words, the control environment is the foundation on which any internal control system rests. The owners or management of an organisation can introduce numerous controls to ensure that nothing goes wrong, but if everyone ignores them, and management do nothing about that, then the internal control system is not likely to operate very well.

There are various ways that a good control environment can be seen in practice:

- Management communicate and enforce integrity and ethical behaviour
- Management and staff are well trained and competent
- Management operates in a way that promotes control
- The organisation is structured in a way that promotes control
- Authority and responsibility for controls is assigned to people
- Human resources policies promote controls

Size of organisation

The size of an organisation will have an impact on the control environment.

Task 1

In what ways do you think the control environment will be affected by the size of an organisation?

Think about the control environment that might exist in a small organisation such as Bayou Stores Limited, in the sample AAT Case Study at the back of this workbook, and in a large multinational organisation. Review the suggested solutions at the back of this workbook once you have attempted this task.

The risk assessment process

As noted above, the internal control system is all about responding to risks that the company's objectives might not be met.

We have already reviewed the AAT's sample Case Study scenario – Bayou Stores Ltd. By way of example, we can look at Bayou Stores Ltd and conclude that it has the following risks with regard to the three identified business objectives:

1   **Reporting accurately** – The owner and most of the accounts team have no formal accounting qualifications and therefore no knowledge of reporting requirements. Also, record keeping is poor and there is no central accounting system.

2   **Operating effectively** – The accounts team are not all in the office at the same time, all are part time and work different days. The owner has recently been absent from work at short notice without adequate cover. If he were to become ill (or if members of the accounts team were to) there is no adequate cover. The business operates with few formal controls and is based on trust in the integrity of staff.

3   **Keeping within applicable laws and regulations** – The business sells many items that are regulated (for example food and cleaning chemicals), but the owner is not a legal expert in this area. Also there is no expert in accounting and payroll regulations and no person responsible for ensuring the business remains up to date with regulations and law.

These are not the only business risks Bayou faces.

All organisations will have some sort of process (not necessarily formal) for assessing the risks it might face and then implementing strategies (controls) to mitigate the risks.

Going back to the risks identified at Bayou, we can now review the actions the owner might have taken in respect of the risks.

1   **Reporting properly** – No formal accounting qualifications are held by the owner or staff – this used to be partly mitigated by the use of a third party to complete the payroll (a highly regulated function), but this is no longer the case. The owner is keen to support staff who wish to train and obtain qualifications but leaves them to organise this themselves.

2   **Operating properly** – The owner left signed cheques to be used during his absence, so that suppliers and staff could continue to be paid, and has now employed one full time member of staff in the accounts department.

3   **Keeping the law** – Very little has been done here according to the scenario. It would be expected that the owner is experienced in some of the regulations affecting the business but this has to be implied, it is not explicit. The scenario does mention that the company has a firm of accountants, Pearl & Johnson, and it could be that they provide appropriate advice to it regarding accounting regulations and payroll law.

Size and type of organisation

Clearly the risks facing a business will be different from one organisation to another and will also be affected by whether a company is large or small and whether it operates in a highly regulated industry or not.

In terms of risk assessment, it may be the case that a smaller organisation tends to do this with the assistance of external advisers. For example, a small organisation may be reliant on the business advice that auditors might give in conjunction with their audit, whereas a larger organisation will rely more on internal staff and may even employ people specifically to assess risks to the business.

Task 2

We are now going to look at another organisation, Metal Extrusions Midlands Limited (MEM).

MEM is a family business which is 80 years old. It has 6 family members on the board of directors, four of whom are active in the business. It employs 50 staff; 40 in manufacturing, 10 in administration. The administration department includes a finance department with a staff of five, including a financial controller. The financial controller is a qualified accountant and is not on the board of directors. None of the directors has any accounting skills.

MEM produces metal extrusions, which is a highly mechanised operation. It has always carried out its operations in the same factory. The factory and its machinery are very old. MEM made a significant investment in new machinery in 1954. There have been few developments in metal extrusion since that time. However, the company has been experiencing competition in recent years from a new company set up by two disgruntled former employees.

MEM has several suppliers of metals and the other materials required for production. There are two major suppliers, one of which is British and the other is French. The company purchases 30% of its metal raw materials from the French supplier, which insists on invoicing and being paid in Euros.

What business risks can you identify, particularly with regard to the business objectives of (1) reporting accurately (2) operating effectively and (3) keeping within applicable laws and regulations?

Control activities

CONTROL ACTIVITIES are the policies and procedures that help ensure that management objectives are carried out.

There are a variety of control activities that can be used by an organisation:

- Performance reviews – comparing budgets to actual performance

- Information processing – checking that transactions have been processed accurately, completely and have been appropriately authorised.

- Physical controls – controls over the physical security of assets

- Segregation of duties – making sure that a number of people are involved in recording each transaction to minimise opportunity for fraud and error.

The precise control activities used will depend on the business and its risks. However, there are some common control activities that are used in many organisations, and we shall look at these in more detail when we look at sales, purchases and wages.

Control activities may include the following:

Approval and control of documents

Transactions should be approved by an appropriate person, for example, overtime should be approved by departmental heads.

Controls over computerised applications

These may be general controls (see below) or application controls which may be built into the system (see below).

Controls over arithmetical accuracy

For example, when invoices are raised or received, a staff member should ensure that the invoice adds up correctly.

Maintaining control accounts and trial balances

You should know from your accounting studies that these can be useful in ensuring that mistakes have not been made in the financial records. For example, some errors will result in a trial balance not balancing.

Reconciliations

Reconciling two different sources of information, such as a bank statement and a cashbook, or a purchase ledger account and a statement from the supplier can also highlight if errors have occurred.

Comparing assets to records

Again, this can identify where errors have been made in recording transactions. For example, staff might compare non-current assets owned by the organisation to those recorded as owned in the non-current asset register or cash in the petty cash tin to the amount shown in the petty cash book.

Restricting access

A good way of restricting errors and particularly the fraud or theft is to restrict access to assets and financial records – for example, by locking receipts in a safe until they go to the bank, having codes to unlock the cash tills and locking the stores where inventory is kept.

Application computer controls

APPLICATION CONTROLS are controls relating to the transactions and standing data relevant to each computer-based accounting system

Controls can be found over **input** to the computer (covering completeness, accuracy and authorisation) **processing** and **standing data**.

For completeness, the person inputting the data might check processed output to source documents on a one to one basis, or might check the number of transactions processed with the number of original documents. There might be an agreement of the total value of the amount processed (a batch total) between the source documents and the total input to the computer.

For accuracy, the computer might have programmed controls to check the plausibility of information being put into certain fields. For example, some fields might be wrong if they were a negative number, or the VAT field might have to be a sensible percentage (20% or 5%) of the total field. Invoice numbers might have to have a letter as well as number values to be valid. Scrutinising output will also help to check accuracy.

Checks over authorisation will be manual – checking to see if the source documentation input has been evidenced as authorised by suitable personnel.

Controls over processing will be similar to the above. In addition, there may be a control built into a programme that warns the user if they try to log out before processing is finished.

Controls over standing data will involve regular reviews of the data to ensure that it is correct and controls like hash totals (for example, of number of personnel on the payroll) to ensure no unauthorised amendments have been made.

General computer controls

GENERAL COMPUTER CONTROLS are controls other than application controls relating to the computer environment. They aim to establish a framework of overall control over the computer information system's activities to provide a reasonable level of assurance that the overall objectives of internal controls are achieved.

Controls will exist over developing computer applications, preventing unauthorised changes to applications, testing genuine changes when they are made, and preventing applications being used by the wrong people at the wrong time.

General computer controls include matters of security – limiting access to computers or computer programmes, both physically (by locking them up) and by using passwords, or creating back ups of important files and then keeping them safe – and procedures over development and testing – isolating development and testing, obtaining approval.

Segregation of duties is also an important general control over computers – as other users of the same programmes would notice unauthorised changes to programmes.

Size of an organisation

Control activities are likely to be similar, regardless of the size of the organisation. However, the personnel involved in carrying out control activities may vary. We have already mentioned in the context of the control environment that in smaller organisations, management may be more involved in actually implementing control activities.

Segregation of duties can be a serious problem for small organisations, where often there are insufficient staff to allow proper segregation between duties to occur.

Task 3

Look back to the descriptions of the information systems at Bayou Stores Ltd. What do you think of the degree of segregation of duties operating in these systems?

Think about what is appropriate to an organisation such as Bayou which is small and with limited finance staff. Could further segregation be implemented? Think this through carefully and then review the suggested answers at the back of this workbook.

Monitoring of controls

MONITORING OF CONTROLS is necessary to assess the quality of internal control performance over time.

In many entities, this is a function that is performed by the internal audit department. If there is no internal audit department, it would be done as a matter of course by departmental heads – for example, the sales director is likely to become aware of deficiencies of controls in the sales cycle because it means his department does not function as well as it might.

Size of the organisation

The personnel monitoring the controls will differ depending on the size of the organisation. For example, a small organisation is unlikely to have an internal audit department. In addition, monitoring of controls is likely to be less formal in a smaller organisation.

Limitations of internal control systems

However good any single element of an internal control system is, it can never be perfect, due to certain inherent limitations. The key limiting factors are the fact that people make mistakes and may not operate controls properly in error, and also that people can deliberately circumvent control systems if they want to defraud the organisation.

SALES SYSTEMS

We have looked at internal controls at some length. Now we are going to look at the types of controls that will be found in sales systems and the risks that they are designed to address.

Control objectives in the sales system

Task 4

Think for a moment about what the aims of an internal control system over sales might be, and what risks it might be aiming to mitigate. In doing so, you might find it helpful to think through the stages of the sales process – for both credit and cash sales. It might be helpful to think about Bayou Stores Ltd, the example Case Study at the back of this workbook. How does their current sales system operate and what risks are there? When you have thought it through, read through the next section, which gives you some examples of controls.

Here we are focusing mainly on the risk of credit sales. When an organisation is making cash sales, no credit is granted, and often there is no formal order as the customer chooses and pays for goods which are available. Risks associated with cash sales are more in respect of the cash element which is discussed at the end.

Orders and extending credit

- An organisation should only supply goods to customers who are likely to pay for them (**risk** – the organisation loses goods of value and does not receive value in return). This is often termed as only selling to customers with a good credit rating.

- An organisation should encourage customers to pay promptly (**risk** – the organisation loses the value of being able to use the money in their business or interest on the money in the bank due to late payment).

- An organisation should record orders correctly (**risk** – the organisation sends the wrong goods to the customer causing added cost or risk of loss of the customer).

- An organisation should fulfil orders promptly (**risk** – the organisation loses custom).

Despatching and invoicing goods

- An organisation should record all goods it sends out (**risk** – goods are sent out and not invoiced, and the organisation loses money).

- An organisation should correctly invoice all goods and services sold (**risk** – insufficient is charged and the organisation loses money).

- An organisation should only invoice goods it has sent out (**risk** – organisation charges for goods in error and loses custom).

- An organisation should only issue credit notes for a valid reason (**risk** – organisation issues credit notes incorrectly and loses money).

Recording and accounting for sales, credit control

- An organisation should record all invoiced sales in its accounting records (sales ledger and general ledger) (**risks** – sales are not recorded and wrongly omitted from financial statements, and payment is not chased as sale was never recorded).

- An organisation should record all credit notes in its accounting records (**risks** – as above, financial statements likely to be misstated and potential to lose custom by chasing cancelled debts).

- An organisation should record all invoiced sales in the correct sales ledger accounts (**risks** – losing custom by chasing the wrong customer for the debt and not receiving the money from the correct customer).

- An organisation must ensure that invoices are recorded in the sales ledger in the correct time period (**risk** – errors in the financial statements due to counting both the sale and the related inventory (stock) as assets or counting neither).

- An organisation must identify debts for which payment might be doubtful (**risk** – organisation fails to take action until it is too late to retrieve the debt and, in the worst case, organisation wrongly records bad debts as assets in the financial statements).

Receiving payment (cash)

- An organisation should record all money received (**risk** – the money could be stolen or lost, custom could be lost through chasing payments already made by the customer, the financial statements are likely to be misstated).

- An organisation should bank all money received (**risk** – the money could be stolen or lost (with consequences as above), the organisation loses out on interest that could be being made on receipts).

- An organisation should safeguard money received in the period until it is banked (**risk** – money may be stolen in the interim period).

Task 5

For each of the objectives given in bullet points above, can you think of a procedure (a control) which will help achieve the objective? When you have thought it through, read through the next section, which gives you some examples of controls.

Controls in the sales system

We shall list some examples of controls in the sales system relating to the objectives outlined above, but before we do, it is relevant to emphasise the importance of segregation of duties in a sales system.

Task 6

Which stages of the sales system do you feel ought to be dealt with by different staff members, and why? Read through the following text to see the answer.

It is possible that a person could create a false customer in order to steal the organisation's inventory (stock) and then not pay for it. This would only be possible if the same person were in charge of orders and credit control/accounts receivable (sales ledgers).

There are two key potential frauds with regard to the receipt of cheques and/or cash from customers. First, a staff member may intercept cheques when they arrive at the organisation and steal them before they are recorded. Second, a staff member may steal cheques and/or cash and misallocate them to the accounts receivable (sales ledger) records (in other words, make it look as if the customer is further behind in payment than he actually is on an ongoing basis). Such a fraud may not be discovered as the customer may never appear behind enough in payments to be chased for overdue debts.

In order to prevent such frauds, several people should be involved in dealing with cheque and/or cash receipts.

Orders and extending credit

- Credit terms offered to customers should be authorised by senior personnel and reviewed regularly

- Credit checks should be carried out on new customers

- Changes in customer data (for example, their address) should be authorised by senior personnel

- Orders should only be accepted from customers with no existing payment problems
- Order documents should be sequentially numbered so that 'false sales' can be traced

Despatching and invoicing goods

- Despatch of goods should be authorised by appropriate personnel and checked to order documents
- Despatched goods should be checked for quality and quantity
- Goods sent out should be recorded
- Records of goods sent out should be agreed to customer orders, despatch notes and invoices
- Despatch notes should be sequentially numbered and the sequence should be checked regularly
- Returned goods should be checked for quality
- Returned goods should be recorded on goods returned notes
- Customers should sign despatch notes as proof of receipt
- Invoices should be prepared using authorised prices and quantities should be checked to despatch notes
- Invoices should be checked to ensure they add up correctly
- Credit notes should be authorised by appropriate personnel
- Invoices and credit notes should be pre-numbered and the sequence should be checked regularly
- Inventory records should be updated from goods sent out records
- Sales invoices should be matched with signed delivery notes and sales orders
- Orders not yet processed should be regularly reviewed

Recording and accounting for sales, credit control

- Sales invoice sequence should be recorded and spoilt invoices recorded and destroyed
- Sales receipts should be matched with invoices
- Customer remittance advices should be retained
- Sales returns and price adjustments should be recorded separately from the original sale
- Procedures should exist to record sales in the correct period

- Receivables statements should be prepared regularly
- Receivables statements should be checked regularly
- Receivables statements should be safeguarded so they cannot be amended before they are sent out
- Overdue accounts should be reviewed and followed up
- Write off of bad debts should be authorised by appropriate personnel
- The accounts receivable control account should be reconciled regularly

Receiving payment (cash)

- There should be safeguards to protect post received to avoid interception
- Two people should be present at post opening, a list of receipts should be made and post should be stamped with the date opened
- There should be restrictions on who is allowed to accept cash (cashiers or sales people)
- Cash received should be evidenced (till rolls, receipts)
- Cash registers should be regularly emptied
- Tills rolls should be reconciled to cash collections which should then be agreed to cash banked
- Cash shortages should be investigated
- Cash records should be maintained promptly
- There should be appropriate arrangements made when cashiers are on holiday
- Receipts books should be serially numbered and kept locked up
- Cash and cheques should be banked daily
- Paying in books should be compared to initial cash records
- All receipts should be banked together
- Opening of new bank accounts should be restricted to certain personnel and authorised by senior management
- Cash floats held should be limited
- There should be restrictions on making payments from cash received and restricted access to cash on the premises
- Cash floats should be checked by an independent person sometimes on a surprise basis
- Cash should be locked up outside normal business hours

Task 7

What are the objectives of the following controls?

- Credit checks should be run on new customers
- Sales invoices should be sequentially numbered
- Receivable statements should be prepared regularly
- Restrictions on who is allowed to receive cash

You should also run through the lists of controls given in the text above to ensure you can identify the objectives behind each of them.

Task 8

Here is some information relating to sales at XYZ Limited:

Peter receives sales orders in a variety of ways: by telephone, by email and in person. Whenever he receives an order, he notes it in the sales order book. Some orders can be fulfilled from shop inventory (stock), others must be ordered from suppliers.

When an order is delivered, Peter raises a despatch note on his computer. The computer automatically raises an invoice when a despatch note is raised. These documents are printed off and sent to the customer. When the documents are printed, the computer programme automatically updates the sales daybook which is also on the computer.

When customers pay, Peter enters the details of the cheques into the cashbook.

Some of the controls in the system have been highlighted. Some of these are manual controls and others are computerised. For instance, orders are manually recorded in the order book, but sales invoices are automatically listed in the sales daybook as a result of a computer programme.

The system at XYZ Limited is very basic and is far from perfect. Can you recommend any other controls that should exist in the system as outlined above?

List out as many as you can, that are appropriate to XYZ Limited, before reviewing the suggested answers at the back of this workbook.

PURCHASES SYSTEMS

Control objectives in the purchases system

> **Task 9**
>
> Think for a moment about what the aims of an internal control system over purchases might be, and what risks it might be aiming to mitigate. In doing so, you might find it helpful to think through the stages of the purchases process. When you have thought it through, read through the suggestions set out below.

Ordering

- An organisation should only order goods and services that are authorised by appropriate personnel and are for the organisation's benefit (**risk** – the organisation pays for unnecessary or personal goods)

- An organisation should only order from authorised suppliers (**risk** – other suppliers may not supply quality goods or may be too expensive)

Receipt of goods and invoices

- An organisation should ensure that goods and services received are used for the organisation's purposes (**risk** – the organisation may pay for goods/services for personal use)

- An organisation should only accept goods that have been ordered (and appropriately authorised) (**risk** – as above)

- An organisation should record all goods and services received (**risk** – the organisation fails to pay for goods/services and loses suppliers)

- An organisation should ensure it claims all credits due to it (**risk** – organisation pays for goods it does not use

- An organisation should not acknowledge liability for goods it has not received (**risk** – organisation pays for goods it has not received)

Accounting

- An organisation should only make authorised payments for goods that have been received (**risk** – as above)

- An organisation should record expenditure correctly in the accounting records (**risks** – financial statements are misstated, and the organisation does not pay for genuine liabilities)

- An organisation should record credit notes received correctly in the accounting records (**risks** – financial statements are misstated, and the organisation pays for items unnecessarily)

- An organisation should record liabilities in the correct accounts payable (purchase ledger accounts) (**risk** – organisation pays the wrong supplier)

- An organisation should record liabilities in the correct period (**risk** – financial statements are misstated by recording purchase but not inventory or recording inventory, but not the associated liability)

Payments

- An organisation should only make payments to the correct recipients and for the correct amounts which are authorised (risk – organisation pays the wrong supplier)

- An organisation should only pay for liabilities once (risk – the organisation pays more than once and the supplier does not correct the mistake)

Task 10

For each of the objectives given in bullet points above, can you think of a procedure (a control) which will help achieve the objective? When you have thought it through, read through the next section, which gives you some examples of controls.

Controls in the purchases system

We shall list some examples of controls in the purchases system relating to the objectives outlined above, but before we do, it is relevant to emphasise the importance of segregation of duties in a purchases system.

Task 11

Which stages of the purchases system do you feel ought to be dealt with by different staff members, and why? Read through the following text to see the answer.

The key areas of concern are:

A person could order and pay for personal goods through the organisation, so ordering and payment should be separated. The risk of fraud will also be reduced if the person who writes out the cheques is different from the person who signs the cheques.

Ordering

- An organisation should have a central policy for choosing suppliers
- The necessity for orders should be evidenced before orders are authorised
- Orders should only be prepared when purchase requisitions are received from departments
- Orders should be authorised
- Orders should be pre-numbered and blank order forms should be safeguarded
- Orders not yet received should be reviewed
- Supplier terms should be monitored and advantage should be taken of discounts offered

Goods and invoices received

- Goods received should be examined for quality and quantity
- Goods received should be recorded on pre-numbered goods received notes
- Goods received notes should be compared with purchase orders
- Supplier invoices should be checked to orders and goods received notes
- Supplier invoices should be referenced (numerical order and supplier reference)
- Supplier invoices should be checked for prices, quantities, calculations
- Goods returned should be recorded on pre-numbered goods returned notes
- There should be procedures for obtaining credit notes from suppliers

Accounting

- Purchases and purchase returns should be promptly recorded in daybooks and ledgers
- The accounts payable (purchase ledger) should be regularly maintained
- Supplier statements should be compared with accounts payable
- Payments should be authorised and only made if goods have been received
- The accounts payable (purchase ledger) control account should be reconciled to the list of balances

- Goods received but not yet invoiced at the year end should be accrued separately

Payments

- Cheques should be requisitioned and requests evidenced with supporting documentation

- Cheque payments should be authorised by someone other than a signatory

- There should be limits on the payment amount individual staff members can sign for

- Blank cheques should never be signed

- Signed cheques should be despatched promptly

- Payments should be recorded promptly in the cashbook and ledger

- Cash payments should be limited and authorised

Task 12

What are the objectives of the following controls?

- The necessity for orders should be evidenced
- Supplier invoices should be matched to goods received
- Supplier statements should be compared with accounts payable
- Blank cheques should never be signed

You should also review the list of all the controls given above and ensure that you understand what the objectives of the controls are.

WAGES SYSTEMS

Control objectives in the wages system

Task 13

Think for a moment about what the aims of an internal control system over wages and salaries might be, and what risks it might be aiming to mitigate. In doing so, you might find it helpful to think through the stages of paying wages and salaries. When you have thought it through, read through the next section, which gives you some examples of controls.

Setting wages and salaries

- An organisation should only pay employees for work they have done (**risk** – the organisation overpays)

- An organisation should pay employees the correct gross pay, which has previously been authorised (**risk** – the organisation overpays)

Recording wages and salaries

- An organisation should record gross pay, net pay, and relevant deductions correctly in the payroll records (**risk** – organisation may make incorrect payments to staff/tax offices and financial statements may be misstated)

- An organisation should record payments made in the bank and cash records and general ledger (**risk** – financial statements may be misstated)

Paying wages and salaries

- An organisation should pay the correct employees (**risk** – angry, unpaid workforce and/or the organisation pays the wrong people)

Deductions

- An organisation should ensure all deductions have been properly calculated and authorised (**risk** – breaking the law, incorrect pension contributions)

- An organisation should ensure they pay the correct amounts to taxation authorities (**risk** – breaking the law and incurring fines)

Task 14

For each of the objectives given in bullet points above, can you think of a procedure (a control) which will help achieve the objective? When you have thought it through, read through the next section, which gives you some examples of controls.

Controls in the wages system

We shall list some examples of controls in the wages system relating to the objectives outlined above, but before we do, it is relevant to emphasise the importance of segregation of duties in a purchases system.

Task 15

Which stages of the wages system do you feel ought to be dealt with by different staff members, and why? Read through the following text to see the answer.

Where there is no segregation of duties it would be possible for the person responsible for the wages system to authorise an inappropriate salary for himself, or enter someone who is not an employee onto the payroll.

Setting wages and salaries

- Personnel records should be maintained and referred to when calculating wages and salaries

- Engaging employees, setting rates of pay, changing rates of pay, overtime, non-statutory deductions from pay and advances of pay should all be authorised and recorded

- Changes in personnel should be recorded

- Hours worked should be recorded, time should be clocked

- Hours worked should be reviewed

- Wages should be reviewed against budget

Recording wages and salaries

- Payroll should be prepared, checked and approved before payments

Paying wages and salaries

- Wage cheque for cash payments should be authorised
- Cash should be kept securely
- Identity of staff should be verified before payment
- Distributions of cash wages should be recorded
- Bank transfer lists should be prepared and authorised
- Bank transfer lists should be compared to the payroll

Deductions from pay

- Separate employees' records should be maintained

- Total pay and deductions should be reconciled month on month

- Costs of pay should be compared to budgets

- Gross pay and total tax deducted should be checked to returns to the tax authorities

---

Task 16

What are the objectives of the following controls?

- Changes in personnel should be recorded
- The wage cheque for cash payments should be authorised
- Costs of pay should be compared to budgets

You should also review the list of all the controls given above and ensure that you understand what the objectives of the controls are.

INTERNAL AUDIT

Internal audit is a function within an organisation that is independent from the managers. This independence is vital as one of the duties of the internal audit function is to review and test internal controls that management have implemented, and to make recommendations to improve them.

The internal audit department will usually report to an audit committee, which for large organisations will include non-executive directors of the organisation.

Many smaller organisations will not have an internal audit department and may outsource the internal audit function to third parties such as their external auditors.

Internal auditors are primarily concerned with improving internal controls. They do this by performing internal audits of various functions within the organisation. They will look at whether the policies and processes in place are designed and operating effectively and make recommendations to improve them.

Internal auditors are also an important tool in risk management in an organisation. They will monitor and evaluate the organisation's risk management processes, and whether these processes protect the owners of the organisation in terms of their investment within it. For example they will review how the accounting systems of the organisation are kept secure, free from error and backed up in case of a system crash.

Internal auditors will also use risk assessment to review which areas of the organisation are at the greatest risk of a loss of controls and prioritise their activities accordingly. A typical internal audit project will include the following processes:

1. Decide and communicate the scope and objectives of the audit

2. Review and map the relevant area of the organisation. This could include interviews with staff as well as documenting systems and processes with tools such as flowcharts

3   Ascertain the key risks in the area under review

4   Identify the current controls in place

5   Test that the controls are effective, by identifying a sample of the controls to test, and then adjusting the sample based on the results of the testing

6   Document the work done and report to management with recommendations to improve

7   Follow up to ensure that the recommendations have been implemented appropriately

REPORT

When completing this section of your report you will need to complete a review of the internal control systems in place within the area of the accounting system that you have chosen to evaluate. This could include reviewing recent internal audit reports if appropriate.

This may have already been part completed as part of your system SWOT analysis (covered in Chapter 4). Remember that controls include system controls, manual controls, personnel controls and accounting controls.

Start a new section in your report entitled **Internal Controls and an Analysis of Fraud** and write a summary of the current controls in place. Depending on the size of your organisation there may have been visits by the internal audit department. If this is the case then include the results of recent visits in your review (and put a copy of relevant reports, if your manager approves this, in your appendices).

From this review of controls you should highlight weaknesses in the current controls, and be able to include recommendations to improve them in your recommendations sub section. Remember that all weaknesses identified must be addressed by recommendations.

Checklist

- Complete a review of the current controls in place within the organisation and or the chosen system

- Include a review of recent internal audit reports if appropriate

- Start a new section of your report entitled Internal Controls and an Analysis of Fraud

- Write a summary under a sub heading Internal systems of control

- Include any documents reviewed in the appendices if possible

- Make recommendations to improve the current controls, where appropriate

- Write short, individually numbered paragraphs

- Write only in the third person

Case Study Advice

Within the case study you will need to review the internal controls in place within the organisation and also the accounting system, or part of the accounting system you have chosen to investigate.

If the specific information contained within the scenario is lacking in detail then supplement it with your own research or knowledge of the work place (for example, you may need to research good controls that should be in place within a purchase ledger system) and discuss this with your assessor if unsure.

In the sample answer in the back of this workbook we have included a range of issues relating to the internal controls at Bayou, from across the accounting system. Depending on the scenario you are using you may wish to focus on one section of the accounting system in particular.

One way to review the controls in place is to review the critical incidents that have occurred. For example when the owner, John Bayou, went to sign some cheques as he was about to take some leave, he found the drawer the book was kept in unlocked. This shows that the internal control in place – that the book was kept in a locked drawer – was not working effectively.

FAQS

1   **My organisation has good controls, how can I complete this section?** – Within this section you are investigating the controls in place and analysing them to determine whether they are adequate or not. From this you can conclude as to whether there are recommendations to make to improve the controls. If you conclude that there are no recommendations to be made because good controls exist then this is acceptable, but unlikely!

2   **How can I research possible controls that should be in my chosen system?** – One way of doing this is to work backwards, start at the current controls in place and then investigate what they could possibly be in place to prevent. You could also search the Internet for examples of your chosen system and controls. i.e. you could search for 'examples of purchase ledger controls'. You could also look at critical incidents that have occurred that have highlighted a lack of controls, or that controls are not being implemented, such as the cheque book incident in Bayou.

3   **My organisation does not have an internal audit department – How do I cover this in my report?** – You do not need to worry if your organisation does not have an internal audit department. In the sample case study, Bayou Stores Limited, there is no such department due to the size and the ownership of the organisation. This section's focus is on internal controls, and this can still be covered.

4   **My organisation has an internal control department but they will not allow me to review its recent reports – is this a problem?** – no, you can still complete your own review of the internal controls in place in your chosen part of the accounting system and make recommendations to improve them.

5   **Any recommendations I come up with are never going to be implemented by my organisation so what should I do?** – This does not matter. The outcome of the ICAS paper should be a professional management report making recommendations to improve the organisation. They do not have to be implemented and while it is hoped that they would at least be reviewed and considered by management this does not actually have to happen.

chapter 6:
ANALYSIS OF FRAUD

chapter coverage 📖

In this chapter we will look at a definition of fraud and provide examples of fraud that might take place within an accounting system.

We will then discuss the general controls that might be in place to prevent or detect fraud and set out the compilation of a fraud matrix which helps to determine the risk to an organisation, and its systems, of fraud.

We will then look at specific examples of accounting systems that are at risk of fraud and the controls that might be in place to prevent them, namely; payroll fraud, purchase ledger fraud and sales ledger fraud.

We will then look at the effect that fraud might have on the organisation together with the action an organisation might take on discovering fraud.

We will then cover fraud in your report, perhaps adding to the SWOT analysis already prepared as part of Chapter 4.

Finally we will include tips for those writing their report from the AAT Case Study scenario.

LEARNING OUTCOMES

PIC 2.3 – Explain methods that can be used to detect fraud within an accounting system

PIC 2.4 – Explain the types of controls that can be put in place to ensure compliance with statutory or organisational requirements

PIC 3.1 – Identify weaknesses in accounting systems

- Potential for errors
- Exposure to possible fraud

PIC 3.2 – Explain how an accounting system can support internal control

EAS 1.4 – Identify potential areas of fraud arising from a lack of control within the accounting system and grade the risk

EAS 2.2 – Identify the effects that any recommended changes would have on the users of the system

EAS 2.3 – Enable individuals who operate accounting systems to understand how to use the system to fulfil their responsibilities

WHAT IS FRAUD?

Fraud is deception of some sort which in the situation of a commercial organisation will involve either:

- Misappropriation of assets
- Misstatement of the financial statements

Misappropriation of assets

In its simplest form, this is the theft of assets such as cash or inventory. However there is a variety of different and subtle ways in which this can be accomplished:

- Theft of cash
- Theft of inventory
- Teeming and lading
- Fictitious employees
- Fictitious suppliers
- Fictitious customers
- Collusion with customers
- Collusion with suppliers
- Receipt of invoices for bogus supply of goods or services
- Disposal of assets

Misstatement of the financial statements

In this type of fraud the financial statements are deliberately manipulated in order to falsify the position of the company. This could be by over-stating assets or profits or by under-stating the results and the profits.

Examples of this type of fraud are:

- Over-valuation of inventory
- Not writing off irrecoverable (bad) debts
- Manipulation of depreciation charges
- Fictitious sales
- Understating expenses

These lists are not exhaustive, you should try to think of any possibilities of fraud within your chosen system.

Task 1

Reading through the sample Case Study at the back of this work book consider all the probable frauds that could occur within the accounts department of Bayou Stores Ltd – even if the controls currently in place make such a fraud unlikely. List as many as you can.

FRAUD CONTROLS

There are many different controls that can be used within organisations to prevent fraud. One key point to note however is that the controls in place must be appropriate to the organisation, taking into account such factors as its ownership, size, staffing etc.

Fraud controls can be grouped into the following categories:

Staff controls – such as supervision, segregation of duties, good recruiting processes (including the following up of references), training and membership of professional bodies.

Management controls – such as effective, well trained managers, authorisation of journals, control limits on expenditure and purchases and authorisation levels for activities. This would also include an internal control or audit role.

Physical controls- such as keeping asset registers or assets under lock and key, access controls to offices and other places of work. Also controlling access to systems as discussed in Chapter 4.

General controls – such as double checking calculations, reporting on exceptions, signing for wages received and rules and procedures in place for staff.

The fraud matrix

A FRAUD MATRIX is a useful tool to assist organisations with investigating the potential for fraud within a system, and analysing the controls currently in place to prevent them. The matrix then grades the potential for fraud, according to risk. Although this is subjective, it enables a risk based approach to improving controls that are appropriate to the organisation under investigation.

The risk to the organisation is graded perhaps 1 = low and 5=high and then possible improvements to the controls for all high and or medium activities can be recommended.

A simple matrix is set out below.

Potential Fraud	Controls currently in place	Risk to the organisation	Implications	Improvement Identified
1				
2				
3				
4				
5				

To assist you with adequately investigating the fraud controls in place within your chosen organisation you will be expected to complete a fraud matrix, preferably on the part of your system that you have chosen to investigate within Chapter 4. The matrix would be placed in the appendices to your report and the body of the report would include a section summarising your findings, with reference to the appendix, and make recommendations to improve the current controls.

To ensure you cover this section to the required sufficiency you should ensure that you include at least 5 potential frauds in your research.

BPP
LEARNING MEDIA

Task 2

Potential Fraud	Controls currently in place	Risk to the organisation	Implications	Improvement identified
1.				
2.				
3.				
4.				
5.				

Taking 5 of the potential frauds analysed in Task 1 construct a fraud matrix, to detail the current controls in place, the implications of fraud to the organisation, the risk to Bayou Stores Limited and recommendations to improve the controls. Ensure the recommendations you make are appropriate to the organisation.

EXAMPLES OF FRAUD

In this section we will review specific examples of fraud that might take place within certain accounting systems, namely:

- Accounts receivable (sales ledger) fraud
- Accounts payable (purchase ledger) fraud
- Payroll fraud

We will also consider examples of the types of controls an organisation might put in place to prevent them.

Examples of accounts receivable fraud

Fraud within the accounts receivable (sales ledger) system is possible because the system involves the receipt of money, especially where this is in the form of cash, from customers for goods or services sold to them. Examples of such frauds might be:

- Stolen cash receipts – cash received is not recorded in the ledgers and is instead taken by employees.

- Overcharging on sales – goods sold are overcharged, with employees keeping the additional amount received from customers.

- Inflating customer orders – with additional goods being retained by employees for own use or to sell on privately.

- Writing off debts – writing off amounts owed and then possibly also keeping any payments made.

- Raising credit notes to reduce amounts owed and then keeping part of any payment made.

One of the controls in place to prevent such examples of fraud might be good company records of goods sold with reconciliations to actual inventory in place.

Task 3

Considering each of the potential accounts receivable frauds identified above suggest a suitable control that might reduce the risk of fraud for a medium sized organisation.

What other, more general, examples of controls can you suggest to reduce the risk of accounts receivable fraud?

Examples of accounts payable fraud

Fraud within the accounts payable (purchase ledger) system is possible because the system includes the ability to order goods from suppliers and then to make payments. Possible examples include:

- Ordering goods for own use – and then paying for them through the organisation's accounts payable

- Fictitious suppliers – making payments to suppliers that do not exist using personal bank accounts to receive the money.

- Paying for genuine goods, but instead of paying suppliers paying the money into personal bank accounts.

- Teeming and Lading – paying into private bank accounts payments owed to suppliers, and then using later payments to pay to the original suppliers and so on, constantly using funds allocated to alternative suppliers to pay off the earlier debts, with the hope that this will hide that an amount of money owed has not been paid.

One of the controls in place to prevent such examples of fraud would be segregation of duties with organisations not allowing the same member of staff to place orders with suppliers, book in goods received and then process payments to them.

Task 4

Considering each of the potential accounts payable frauds identified above suggest a suitable control that might reduce the risk of fraud for a medium sized organisation.

What other, more general, examples of controls can you suggest to reduce the risk of accounts payable fraud?

Examples of payroll fraud

There is a risk of fraud within the payroll system because the system involves the payment of money that could be misappropriated. Examples of such fraud might be:

- Ghost employees – having more employees on the payroll than physically exist within the organisation.

- Overstating overtime pay – paying for more hours than physically worked

- Increasing hourly rate / salary – paying a higher hourly rate or salary than contracted for

- False expense reimbursement claims – expenses are often paid through payroll and false claims may be processed this way

- Keeping employees on the payroll once they have resigned – and amending the bank details so that the pay is paid into own / third parties account

- Unofficially recruiting new staff – and adding their details to the payroll system

One of the controls in place to prevent such a fraud would be the competence and integrity of the person completing the payroll. This might be strengthened if that person has a payroll or accounting qualification, and is a member of a professional body such as the AAT. There are other, more specific, controls that can be put in place to lower the risk of payroll fraud.

Task 5

Considering each of the potential payroll frauds identified above, suggest a suitable control that might reduce the risk of fraud for a medium sized organisation with 2 payroll staff.

What other, more general, examples of controls can you suggest to reduce the risk of payroll fraud?

THE IMPACT OF FRAUD ON THE ORGANISATION

Fraud impacts an organisation in a variety of ways:

Financial – fraud involves the theft of funds or assets from an organisation. This in turn affects its profitability and the owner's investment in the organisation. It can also impact a company's share price.

Reputation – exposure of fraud can affect an organisation's reputation with all internal and external stakeholders. This in turn could lead to loss of business.

Employee morale – the trust of existing employees could be damaged. Future recruitment and retention of staff might also be affected.

Depending on the organisation type the owner(s) of the organisation that will suffer as a result of fraud will be different, and may take different actions on discovery of fraud taking place.

In the UK the Serious Fraud Office (SFO) offer advice and guidance to organisations on dealing with suspected fraud and offer a service for organisations and employees to report serious or complex fraudulent activities.

www.sfo.gov.uk

Less serious fraud can be reported to Action Fraud www.actionfraud.org.uk

REPORT

When completing this section of your report you will need to complete an analysis of the risk of fraud within your organisation or part of the system chosen. This will include completing a fraud matrix.

This may have already been part completed as part of your system SWOT analysis (covered in Chapter 4).

In the section of your report entitled Internal Controls and Analysis of Fraud write a summary of the analysis of fraud and risks, under a sub heading – **Analysis of Fraud**. Make reference to your fraud matrix, constructed from your analysis of possible frauds, in your appendices.

From this analysis of the risk of fraud you should highlight weaknesses (sometimes referred to as deficiencies) in the current controls, and be able to include recommendations to improve them. Remember that all weaknesses identified must be addressed by recommendations.

Checklist

- Complete a Fraud Matrix on your chosen system or part of a system

- Grade the risk to the organisation of each fraud occurring

- Put the Matrix in the appendices

- Write a summary in the main report

- Refer to the appendices

- Make recommendations to improve the current controls, where appropriate

- Write short, individually numbered paragraphs

- Write only in the third person

Case Study Advice

As with the accounting system section you should pick one area of the Case Study scenario to cover for this section.

If the specific information contained within the scenario is weak then supplement it with your own research or knowledge of the work place (for example, you may need to research the types of fraud that might occur within a purchase ledger system) and discuss this with your assessor if unsure.

FAQS

1   **My company has good controls and fraud is unlikely, how can I complete this section?** – Within this section you are investigating all the possible frauds that could occur and analysing the current controls to determine whether they are adequate or not. From this you can conclude as to whether there are recommendations to make to improve the controls. If you conclude that there are no recommendations, because good controls exist, then this is acceptable.

2   **Can the fraud risk matrix be included in the body of the report?** – You should keep all tables, charts and diagrams in the appendices to a professional report and make reference to them in the body of the report.

3   **How can I grade the risk of the fraud occurring?** – To do this construct your own, simple, grading system. Perhaps a grade of 1 = low risk of occurring and 5 = high risk of occurring.

4   **How can I research possible frauds in my chosen system?** – One way of doing this is to work backwards, start at the controls in place and then investigate what they could possibly be in place to prevent. You could also research the Internet using a search engine and searching for examples of your chosen system fraud. i.e. you could search for 'examples of accounts payable or purchase ledger fraud'.

5   **Any recommendations I come up with are never going to be implemented by my organisation so what should I do?** – This does not matter. The outcome of the ICAS paper should be a professional management report making recommendations to improve the organisation. The recommendations do not have to be implemented and while it is hoped that they would at least be reviewed and considered by management this does not actually have to happen.

chapter 7:
COST BENEFIT ANALYSIS AND COMPLETING YOUR REPORT

— **chapter coverage** 📖 —

This chapter looks at the requirement that the recommendations made in the report be fully supported by a cost benefit analysis. Such an analysis is an important part of any report that makes recommendations. It helps any decision maker reading the report to understand the costs associated with the implementation of the recommendations and the benefits that will be gained from doing so.

As part of this report you will be expected to explain all or some of your recommendations in terms of the costs and benefits of implementation. How many you justify will depend on how many recommendations you have made. You will be expected to explain and quantify the costs and benefits where possible between those that are tangible, or easy to quantify, and those that are intangible – much harder to quantify. You should also consider the opportunity costs of any actions and this chapter will help you understand how to consider these.

Finally you need to consider the impact of your recommendations, in terms of costs and benefits, on the organisation and its staff, including their training needs and response to change.

COST BENEFIT ANALYSIS

The Cost Benefit Analysis (CBA) takes your recommendations and analyses them in terms of the costs and benefits to the organisation of implementing them.

Both costs and benefits can be categorised under the headings of tangible and intangible.

Tangible – these are costs and benefits that are easy to value in terms of time and/or money.

For example, if recommending a new computer system then tangible costs would include:

- The cost of the system itself
- The loss of staff time while they are training
- The cost of future licences and improved speed of processing

Wherever possible in your CBA you should include tangible costs with an estimate of them.

You would not be expected to get detailed quotations or information to support your recommendations but you should make estimates as to what the costs will be as this will aid the reader of your report in making any decisions as to whether to implement the recommendations.

Task 1

A firm of accountants has decided to train all new staff in basic bookkeeping as part of their induction programme. What tangible costs might there be to such a decision?

What would your estimates of these costs be? Think of costs not just in terms of money spent but also in relation to time and any other quantifiable measure.

Intangible – these are costs and benefits that are much harder to quantify.

For example a new computer system may: Improve the motivation and morale of staff.

Although happier, more motivated staff may be more efficient resulting in an increase in organisational productivity, this is more difficult to value in monetary terms.

Task 2

What would be the intangible costs of the training outlined in Task 1? Try to jot down as many as you can and then review our suggested answers at the back of this workbook.

For all of the recommendations you make in your report there should be some intangible costs and/or benefits identified.

These do not have to have estimated values assigned to them but as they are often powerful persuaders for implementing a recommendation they should be included so that the decision maker can consider all the issues fully.

Task 3

What tangible and intangible benefits might there be to such training as part of an induction programme for new staff?

Try to think about why an organisation would want to include this training as part of such an programme. When you have listed both tangible and intangible benefits then review the suggested answers at the back of this workbook.

Opportunity cost – another important type of cost to include is the opportunity cost of the recommendation. An opportunity cost can be defined as the value of an activity which has not taken place, because of a decision to do something else.

For example, in the tasks above, the organisation has chosen to send all new staff on a bookkeeping course. When completing the tasks you will (hopefully) have listed both tangible and intangible costs and benefits of this decision. One of the costs we have included in our example answers is an opportunity cost. Can you see which one?

The answer is that the revenue lost, because the new staff are not working for clients and therefore are not generating chargeable hours, is an opportunity cost of the decision. Where possible try to identify the opportunity costs of your recommendations.

REPORT

The Cost Benefit Analysis can either go in your report as a new chapter, before the appendices, or as an appendix in itself.

Which approach you choose may be influenced by the overall word count of the report so far, remember that this does *not* include the appendices.

Whichever approach you choose, ensure your Cost Benefit Analysis is referred to in your executive summary as it is an important part of the overall report (see below).

To complete your Cost Benefit Analysis ensure that you consider at least two or three of your main recommendations and cover both the tangible and intangible costs and benefits of them. Where possible, you should also try to identify opportunity costs and include estimated values for all of your tangible costs and benefits.

Case Study Advice

Within the case study you may not have access to detailed financial information such as staff wages and salaries. In order to complete your CBA you will have to estimate the tangible costs and benefits of the recommendations you have made.

If estimates of costs and benefits are difficult to express in terms of monetary value then ensure you quantify them in other ways such as time.

COMPLETING YOUR REPORT

If you have been following this workbook as you complete your actual report then you should now have completed much of the work required.

This chapter covers the other sections of your report which are necessary in order to pull it together into a completed final report ready for assessment by your assessor.

The sections of the full report are:

- Title Page
- Contents Page
- Terms of Reference
- Executive Summary
- Methodology
- Introduction to the Organisation
- The Accounts Department
- A Review of an Accounting system
- Internal Control and Analysis of Fraud
- Recommendations to Improve
- Cost Benefit Analysis
- Appendices

As you will now have completed the main areas of your report and made some recommendations to improve the organisation's accounting systems and internal controls, we will now look at each of the remaining sections in turn.

Apart from the first two, the title page and the contents page, each must be included as numbered sections to your report with the individual paragraphs numbered as per the guidance in the rest of this workbook.

Title page

The title page of your report should contain a meaningful title, your full name and your AAT student registration number.

A meaningful title might be:

> *A report analysing the Internal Controls in place and Evaluating the 'Accounting System' of XYZ PLC.*

Your title should reflect both the name of your organisation and the system you have chosen to investigate.

The title page should also contain an authenticity statement. This is where you confirm that the work undertaken to complete the report is your own, and unaided and that it is a true reflection of the organisation.

Warning – Completing, by signing and dating, this statement means that you are testifying that the work is your own and unaided. Your report should not include any material copied from sample reports such as the one at the back of this workbook, or from other students' work. Submitting work which is not your own may result in your assessor reporting you to the AAT's conduct and compliance team.

Contents page

This should set out the page and section number of each part of your report. It is also recommended that you include a word count on this page of the total number of words in your report, excluding the appendices.

Most word processing packages include a word count facility. To check the word count in Microsoft Word click on Tools, Word Count and the total number of words will be calculated. Remember not to include your appendices in the word count.

An example contents page would look like this:

Contents		
Section:		**Page:**
1	Terms of Reference	2
2	Executive Summary	3
3	Methodology	4
4	Introduction to the organisation	5
5	The Accounts Department	6
6	A review of the Accounting System	7
7	Internal Control and an Analysis of Fraud	9
8	Recommendations to Improve	11
9	Cost Benefit Analysis	12
10	Appendices	13
Word Count: 4056 words		

Terms of reference

This should be a short section that explains to the reader exactly what the report sets out to do. It explains why it is being written and the areas it covers.

The terms of reference for the ICAS report can also include that you are completing the report as part of your AAT Level 4 Diploma in Accounting studies. This would not be included in a professional business report but is relevant to why you have produced this work and can be included here.

As with the whole report, none of this section should be written in the first person, ie you should not use the words 'I' or 'my'. An example of suitable text is included in the sample report at the back of this Companion.

Methodology

This will show how you planned and investigated your report ie questionnaires, books, internet etc

Executive summary

This is a short, summarised version of the overall report that sets out the main findings for the reader.

Imagine that you have commissioned a report into a possible re-structuring of your company and have recruited some consultants to do this for you – they have produced for you a 10,000 word report detailing their findings, recommendations and rationale behind them.

Although you would probably want to read through the full report at some stage you would also want a summarised version to set the overall scene before you do so, detailing the main recommendations and a brief explanation of why they have been identified.

This is what an executive summary does.

The AAT guidance on the executive summary states that it should be:

'A short (two or three paragraphs only) overview of the report's findings and the benefits that the organisation will gain by following the recommendations within the report'

Therefore in your report it should be no more than 2 – 3 paragraphs long and should summarise your main recommendations and reasons for them.

This does, briefly, repeat the recommendations which you will also include in your main report but this is important to set the scene for your reader before they become involved with the detail.

Your executive summary must also refer to your Cost Benefit Analysis as this is an important part of summarising the overall costs and benefits of the recommendations made.

Other sections

You should now include the other sections of your report as laid out in this text:

- Introduction to the Organisation
- The Accounts Department
- A Review of an Accounting system
- Internal Control and Analysis of Fraud
- Recommendations to Improve
- Cost Benefit Analysis
- Appendices

Ensure that all pages and paragraphs are numbered and that the appendices are also numbered, and referred to in the main report.

The **Appendices** can be split down further to include:

Appendices to the report – eg organisation charts, SWOT analysis, Fraud Matrix etc

Mapping to the standards – Your report is required to be fully mapped to the standards and therefore to the assessment criteria and learning outcomes. In order to do this you require a mapping sheet that sets out all the standards for the two units that make up this paper; Principles of Internal Control and Evaluating Accounting Systems. Next to each criterion list the paragraph numbers that demonstrate that you have shown competence in it. An example mapping is included in our sample report at the back of this workbook.

As you map your work you may find that some of the more technical learning outcomes are not covered fully by your report, for example you may have referred to income statements but not explained their use in decision making.

The AAT have allowed this report to have technical notes in the appendices, if required, to strengthen areas such as this. For advice on how to complete the technical notes see below.

Once your mapping is complete you must then review whether all the standards have been covered by your report. If not then you may need to add to it in order to strengthen it. If you are unsure about this then you should discuss this with your assessor.

Technical Notes – If an assessment criterion is not covered in the report (or not to the depth required by the assessor), then this can be covered within a written explanation included in the appendix.

This allows you to cover some of the more technical learning outcomes of the standards as part of technical notes in the appendix. An example of this is in appendix 4 of our sample report at the back of this workbook.

Please note that this should only be completed by exception, and that the main report should map to, and demonstrate competence in, as many of the standards as possible.

If you are unsure about how to complete the technical notes then you should discuss this with your assessor.

Manager's authenticity statement – where the report has been based on your workplace, the final appendix to include is a manager's authenticity statement. This will confirm that the work is your own and unaided and that the report is a true reflection of the organisation. This must be signed and dated, include your manager's full contact details, and must also be printed on your organisation's headed paper.

ANSWERS TO CHAPTER TASKS

CHAPTER 1   The Basic Principles of ICAS

No tasks

CHAPTER 2   Introduction to the organisation

1   The aims and objectives common to most types of organisation:

- Provide goods and/or services
- Employ staff
- Manage cash flow
- Control internal systems effectively
- Keep expenditure and/or revenue within budgets
- Manage stakeholder expectations
- Efficiency
- Customer satisfaction
- Public reputation

Differences in aims and objectives – public and private sector organisations:

- Public sector – social / ethical issues, provision of service, equality of access to service

- Private sector – sales, profit, share price, survival

Organisation type affects the organisation's approach to all the factors identified above

2   Other factors that affect an organisation might include:

- Customers
- Suppliers
- Employees
- Culture
- The environment within which it operates
- Owners
- Age
- Size
- Strategy

- Market
- Wealth
- Status
- Structure
- Product or service offered
- Skills of the workforce

3   The advantages of a tall organisation structure include:

- Narrow span of control – easier for management to manage a few employees

- Clear management structure

- Clear lines of responsibilities

- Clear lines of control

- Employees can see a clear progression ladder, which can feel more achievable

- Structure suited for larger organisations

The advantages of a flat organisation structure include:

- More freedom and responsibility for employees

- Quicker decision making that is not hindered by many levels of management

- Quicker communication from top to bottom

- Less management cost

- Improved team working

- Less bureaucracy

4   Internal stakeholders include:

- Employees
- Management
- Owners

External stakeholders might include:

- Community groups
- Customers
- Suppliers
- The Government
- Regulatory bodies
- Society
- Payables (creditors)
- Shareholders

- Schools, colleges & universities
- Competitors
- Professional associations
- Industry trade groups
- Landlords

Information needs of internal stakeholders might include all financial and management reports (see chapter 4) plus other ad-hoc and regular reports that meet the stakeholders' needs.

External stakeholders may wish to have some of the information that internal stakeholders have access to but it would not always be in the organisation's best interest to provide it! Organisations can have different approaches to different external stakeholders – often dependent on their individual power and influence over the organisation. Some information may also need to be provided to meet regulatory requirements – e.g. Tax returns.

Organisations meet both the information needs of internal and external stakeholders through effective Management Information Systems (MISs) and this will include accounting systems.

CHAPTER 3   The Accounts Department

1   Advantages of a centralised accounts department include:

- Greater senior management control of the department's activities

- Standard, consistent procedures

- Decisions can be made taking into account the 'big picture' or the organisation as a whole

- The organisation can employ, and benefit from the skills and experience of, more senior, qualified managers and accountants

- In uncertain times the organisation will benefit from strong, central leadership

- Reporting may be quicker and benefit from standard report layouts and central information

The disadvantages of a centralised accounts department might include

- Less decision making, and therefore empowerment of junior staff

- Accountants and managers at a central location may lose touch with the operational side of the organisation, weakening decision making abilities

- Senior management can be tied up making decisions that should be made lower down the organisation

- Communication and interaction between the accounts department and other functions of the organisation my be impaired

- Other parts of the organisation might resent controls being imposed by a central accounting department due to a lack of knowledge and appreciation of the department's requirements

2   To demonstrate what reports could be prepared we have used the sample Case Study scenario at the back of this work book – Bayou Stores limited. At present there seems to be very few, if any, management accounting reports prepared. Those that would benefit the organisation might include:

- A budget
- Variance report – budget to actual sales
- Variance report – budget to actual costs
- Inventory report – values of inventory
- Inventory report – age of inventory
- Profitability reports – different product lines
- Aged debt report
- Overhead costs – apportioned to products sold
- Cash flow forecasts and statements
- Wages and salaries – average employee wage, overtime worked etc

Such reports would provide the owner, John Bayou, with a snapshot of the business and the key financial data that affects its profitability. For each of the above reports you should be able to review the value it would add to John Bayou's decision making regarding the organisation. The more information management and owner have, the better informed decisions they can make. Especially if the information is about a critical area of the business. For example an aged inventory report would enable John to see which products are spending too long on the shelves, and taking up shelf space that other, more saleable products could use. As the goods he sells could also be perishable there could be a risk of inventory going out of date, causing a loss to the business. For your own organisation you can think about critical information that would enable better informed decisions to be made.

3   There are both internal and external stakeholders to the accounts
     department of Bayou Stores Limited:

Stakeholder		Information needs
Internal	Owner – John Bayou	The owner requires accurate financial and management reporting information. He requires a complete set of financial reports including the income statement (profit and loss account) and the statement of financial position (balance sheet) plus management reports as listed as part of the answer to task 2 above. This will enable him to make much better informed decisions regarding the business. It is clear from the scenario that the organisation's cash flow has not been proactively managed, hence the bank is now asking for a reduction in an overdraft that the owner is unaware of. This is a good example where better information would have led to improved decision making.
	Stores staff	They require accurate completion of their wages and salaries. The warehouse supervisors would also benefit from reports such as aged inventory reports to enable them to better manage the warehouse inventory.
	Accounts staff	Each of the accounts staff performs a separate, distinct role with regard to the preparation of the accounts and each is an internal stakeholder to the department as a whole. Each requires data and information plus good communications with each other. The scenario sets out examples where a lack of communication has led to information not being passed on (for example in the case of the payment to the supplier when the accounts receivable clerk did not inform the accounts clerk that the supplier had been paid) and this could lead to payments being made twice and incorrect financial accounts.

Stakeholder		Information needs
External	HM Revenue & Customs	The accounts department are responsible for preparing the information that will lead to the calculation of the tax due to HM Revenue & Customs. This will include national insurance contributions, corporation tax, VAT and PAYE tax and so it will require timely, accurate information in order that the correct tax is paid.
	Customers	The accounts department in Bayou Stores Limited is responsible, through the accounts receivable clerk, for granting credit to new and existing customers. The customers will want information on the credit limit granted to them and also statements regarding how much they owe.
	Suppliers	Suppliers to Bayou Stores Limited are stakeholders to the accounts team through the accounts payable clerk. Suppliers want to be paid accurately, and on time.
	Bank Manager	The manager of the bank of Bayou Stores Limited has identified that the overdraft of the organisation is too large. The bank is a payable (creditor) of the business and will perhaps ask to see accurate cash flow forecasts to enable them to see that the overdraft can be reduced within the time scales set.

There are many information needs not currently being met in Bayou Stores Limited as there is very little financial and management reporting taking place. The above examples set out the information needs of key stakeholders. They also demonstrate where better information could have led to more informed decision making. The owner of the organisation, and perhaps the new senior accounts clerk, requires a full, accurate and timely set of financial and management reports. At present this is not being completed due to a variety of reasons, including the lack of a centralised accounting system.

CHAPTER 4   Accounting systems

1   Advantages of a centralised system might include:

- All data is stored in one central place so greater control
- Improved security
- Staff can all use the same system leading to efficiencies in training etc
- Centralised reporting
- Consistent reporting
- Quicker access to information

Advantages of a decentralised system might include:

- Each individual system can be more relevant to that area of the organisations needs
- Lower risk of errors / breakdowns affecting the whole organisation
- Lower level staff might have more control and autonomy over their system thus improving morale
- Quicker access to information from each, individual system

Bayou Stores Limited is better suited to a centralised system so that all staff can be trained to use one system and can then cover each other's roles or access information if required. It will also enable financial reports to be quickly and easily provided to the owner for management decision making.

2   The advantages of having a user manual for all of the activities that take place within an accounts department include:

- Quick and efficient training of new staff
- Better visibility of the controls in place
- Consistent approach to completing activities
- Easier to rotate staff between roles and responsibilities
- Easier to evaluate staff
- Improved supervisory and management control
- More effective time management

Disadvantages of such an approach might be:

- Increased risk of 'outsiders' being able to operate the system
- Procedures may stifle innovation and improvements to processes
- User manuals take time to complete
- The manuals may become out of date quickly
- The manuals need to be tested to ensure they accurately reflect the systems in place
- Staff often do not conform to manuals, negating the benefits of having them

3 An organisation might put in place the following rules regarding the use and control of passwords.

- Passwords must not be written down

- Passwords must not be shared

- Passwords must be changed regularly

- Passwords must not be generic

- When staff leave, access must be cancelled on the day they leave the department

- Access can only be set up for new staff with management authorisation

- Staff access to different parts of the system must be regularly reviewed

It is important that these types of rules and controls are in place to protect the integrity of the system and the organisation. If one password is used by all staff (generic) then there is little point in using them as the whole system is open to all. This lack of control then increases the risk of errors, from staff using parts of the system they are not trained to, and fraud.

It is also important that new access to the system is controlled so that staff are not granted access to parts of the system they do not require and that as staff leave, their access is cancelled promptly so that they can not continue to use the system, and other staff can not use their passwords. Often organisations make sharing of passwords a disciplinary offence to ensure that controls are maintained.

4   A system flowchart for the accounts payable function might be:

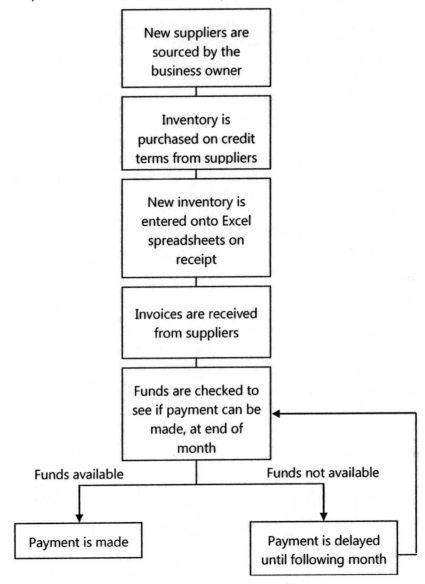

Recommendations to improve the accounts payable and payroll systems might include:

Accounts payables system:	Payroll system:
New suppliers should only be set up on the system after documented approval from the business owner	All managers and supervisors should complete weekly sheets on actual hours worked by staff
An integrated accounts system should be implemented, that shows inventory levels and invoices due for payment. Inventory delivered and invoices received should be entered to this system	Staff should sign in and out of work, with the relevant time noted
Purchase orders should be raised for all inventory purchases, and should be appropriately authorised	All overtime hours should be appropriately authorised by management
Inventory deliveries should be matched to purchase orders on receipt	The Sage payroll system should be used to calculate wages due based on hours worked and authorised
Inventory deliveries should be checked for accuracy and quality on receipt	BACS payments should be implemented for all staff
Invoices should be matched to purchase orders and goods received before payment	If cash and cheque payments are to continue, these should be collected only by the relevant members of staff and signed for on collection
Invoices should be appropriately authorised for payment	Procedures should be in place to cover payroll staff member's absence
Payments to suppliers should follow standard payment terms	

Note: The above improvements are in relation to our interpretation of the accounting system in the scenario. The scenario is not explicit about the type of controls in place regarding some of the activities taking place. We therefore have assumed they are not in place and have included them in our improvements (and in a report they would be reflected in the recommendations made). You might assume that all or some are in place, just not detailed specifically in the scenario. Either approach is fine.

5   An example SWOT analysis for Bayou Stores Limited might include:

Strengths	Weaknesses
■ An open plan accounts office ensures that when staff are in and working with each other they can communicate freely and cover each others work when absent. ■ The cheque book is kept in a locked desk in the office – but see weaknesses. ■ Current inventory system has good detail included ■ Credit reference agency used to decide whether to grant credit ■ Credit control procedures in place ■ Controls re: cash and cheques coming into the office – manual day book then accounts. ■ Staff seem keen to improve systems – Accounts receivable clerk has implemented some initiatives. ■ Cash movement is reduced by using cash to make up wages.	■ As most accounts staff are part time there are often occasions when no one is in the office. Because all staff can access the office and the accounts system with common passwords there is a risk of lack of control. There will also be issues concerning communication between staff as they are not all in the office at the same time. ■ Stand alone computers with no central system means that the system does not produce central, standard reports for key stakeholders ■ Staff, as a whole, are not qualified in accounting which poses a risk of errors and relaxed controls and also a lack of accountability. ■ There appears to be a lack of planning in the work of the accounting team, highlighted by the fact that when the payroll was first bought in house a temping agency was contracted to run it for the first two months. This could have led to errors and inconsistencies in the work, and therefore within the hand over of the system to the payroll clerk once employed. ■ Stores staff are paid in cash which poses a risk of theft ■ Office staff are paid by cheque – there is a risk of cheques being stolen and fraudulently used. ■ Manual calculation of weekly payroll is a weakness as it can lead to errors or fraudulent increases in staff pay. ■ Cash is withdrawn to pay wages – as above, any use of cash

	<ul><li>On at least one occasion the cheque book was accessed by other members of staff as the draw it is kept in was found to be unlocked.</li><li>Staff are not trained in excel and could make errors</li><li>No further check on new credit customers other than credit reference agency</li><li>Manual completion of invoices, on Word, could lead to errors.</li><li>Cash is not counted when removed from the tills on weekdays.</li><li>No petty cash – so no control on cash taken from tills.</li><li>No contingency planning – staff able to take on each others roles when absent.</li><li>Staff can not use each others systems.</li><li>No control on authorisation – signing of blank cheques to cover absence.</li><li>No controls on payments to customers.</li><li>Payments to suppliers are made without checking systems, or informing other staff.</li><li>Lack of controls on staff hours have led to incorrect rotas and staff pay.</li><li>Three weeks pay packets completed in advance – this is a weakness as too much cash was in the office.</li><li>Wages should be completed correctly, not in advance and adjusted later.</li><li>Wages have been handed to staff family members. There is no control that it should only be handed to staff / others with permission.</li></ul>

Opportunities	Threats
▪ There is an opportunity to use one central accounts system on networked computers which will ensure that there is better cover for work when staff are absent and better reporting of key financial data to relevant stakeholders. ▪ There is an opportunity to train staff in accounting and also in the systems they use, making them much more aware of the controls and procedures they should be operating with and also more efficient. ▪ There is an opportunity to train staff in each others roles – perhaps with a back-up member of staff for each. This could motivate staff and also ensure cover during absence.	▪ Having the accounts prepared on Excel poses a risk that errors can be made to the spreadsheets that will not be easily identified, and therefore the inventory and accounting information may be incorrect. ▪ There is a threat to the office and its systems by the common use of one password across the organisation – any staff who wanted to could access the office and the accounting systems. ▪ The lack of formal procedures and control in respect of accounts payable and receivable has led to an overdraft that the bank has asked to be repaid. This is a cash flow threat to the organisation. ▪ There appears to be no back-up taken of the current systems which is a threat as if the systems in use failed key financial data would be lost.

CHAPTER 5   Internal controls

1   A larger organisation might have a set of internal controls, whereas it is unlikely that a smaller organisation will. In a small organisation, senior managers may work closely with operational staff and their attitude to controls will be particularly influential.

2   **Business risks at MEM**

(1)   Reporting properly

The fact that the qualified accountant is not on the board may impair the effectiveness of the board to report properly.

The fact that the company deals in more than one currency increases the risk of errors in the financial statements.

(2) Operating properly

The business is at risk of not operating properly due to out of date machinery.

In addition, the company is facing increased competition from a company which is likely to have more up to date equipment and may have a useful knowledge of MEM's operating practices.

(3) Keeping within the law

The company has a number of employees and must ensure that it satisfies the many legal requirements in relation to its employees.

The company operates from an old building using old machines. It must ensure that it operates within the boundaries of health and safety law as well.

3   There is very little segregation of duties at Bayou Stores Limited and, although the key sales, wages and purchase functions are carried out by different staff, the system would benefit from some segregation being introduced. For example, payments for purchases should be authorised by someone other than Marion. It would be appropriate for the new, full time, senior accounts clerk (you!) to authorise all such payments.

4   The answer follows the question in the chapter text below it.

5   Examples of controls are given in the next section of the chapter.

6   The answer follows the question in the chapter text below it.

7   Credit checks on new customers are to ensure that the customer is a good credit risk and able to pay for goods/services purchased.

Sales invoices should be sequentially numbered to ensure that fictitious sales invoices are not raised (and used to then misappropriate genuine payments for other invoices).

Receivable statements should be prepared regularly to check that the sales ledger has been kept correctly (customers are likely to draw attention to debts that are not genuine) and to encourage trade receivables (debtors) to pay promptly.

There should be restrictions on who is allowed to receive cash for the business to minimise the risk of cash being stolen or lost.

8
- Sales orders should be recorded on pre-numbered documents
- Despatch notes should be checked to sales orders prior to despatch
- The accounts receivable ledger should be written up more frequently to aid credit control
- Accounts receivable ledger should be reviewed frequently to check for irrecoverable (bad) debts
- Someone other than Peter should record and bank receipts

9   The answer follows the question in the chapter text below it.

10 Examples of controls are given in the next section of the chapter.

11 The answer follows the question in the chapter text below it.

12 The necessity of orders should be evidenced so that goods are only purchased for genuine business reasons.

Supplier invoices should be referenced so that they can be recorded in sequence and so that they can be found easily in the event of disputes.

Supplier statements should be compared to the accounts payable ledger to discover errors in recording in the accounts payable ledger and/or to discover whether the company is being charged for genuine liabilities.

Blank cheques should never be signed as this makes it easier for cash to be stolen from the company/spent on goods which are not for business use.

13 The answer follows the question in the chapter text below it.

14 Examples of controls are given in the next section of the chapter.

15 The answer follows the question in the chapter text below it.

16 Changes in personnel should be recorded so that the right employees are paid for work done.

A payroll should be prepared to ensure that employees are paid the correct amounts and the correct deductions are made, and posting to the general ledger can be checked.

A wage cheque for cash payments should be authorised so that cash is not stolen.

Costs of pay should be compared to budgets because any discrepancies observed might reveal errors in calculation or in payments made to staff or leavers inappropriately.

CHAPTER 6   Analysis of fraud

1   Frauds that could occur within the accounts department include:

- Theft of assets – computers or other assets could be stolen by any of the staff within Bayou Stores Limited due to the easy access to the accounts office.

- Overstatement of wages – there are no controls in place to approve actual wages paid to staff, so the wages clerk could overstate wages by either overpaying on hours worked and / or the hourly rate.

- Theft of cash from the office – although cash and wages are kept in the safe there is little control over access to the office and no mention of controls in place when the wage packets are being prepared.

- Theft of cash by overstating the weekly cheque – there is no control between the amount of cash required to complete the wages and the cheque completed to withdraw the cash.

- Theft of cheques – there are few controls in place to store the cheque book securely and it has been found in an unlocked drawer together with blank, signed cheques.

- Overstatement of hours worked – the stores supervisor could add more hours to the staff rotas than physically worked by staff

- Theft of inventory – there is no mention of controls such as inventory counts to prevent the theft of inventory from the warehouse.

- Overpayment of supplier invoices – there is no control to check that cheques prepared to pay suppliers equate to the amount physically owed and invoiced.

- Under recording of goods sold – there are few controls in place to ensure goods purchased are accurately recorded.

- Writing off of debts – there are no controls to ensure that debts from customers are not written off.

- Theft of cash or cheques from the mail – no separate controls are in place to record cash and/or cheques received.

- Theft of cash and/or cheques from tills – the tills are not balanced each evening so there is no accountability for any missing cash and/ or cheques.

- Theft of cash from tills – as there is no formal petty cash system in place and staff take cash from tills to pay for incidental expenses required.

- Theft of wages – in the incident regarding David Singh staff prepared a second wage packet without checking where the original was. Staff could therefore claim two sets of wages for one week.

- Overpayment of suppliers – in a separate incident a supplier was paid without further checks on the amount owed, this could lead to overpayment.

- Theft of wages – in a further separate incident a member of staff's family collected their wages without that staff members consent. Staff could therefore claim two sets of wages for one week.

2   Below we have completed a fraud matrix with suggested improvements to the controls currently in place. It should be noted that there are many possible ways of rectifying identified weaknesses and the ones included within your final report should be relevant to your organisation. For example we could not suggest full segregation of duties within Bayou Stores Limited as there are not enough staff working within the accounts department to make this possible! Also the assessment of risk is purely subjective, based on our knowledge of the organisation and the controls currently in place.

It should also be noted that not all these recommendations may be implemented by the management of the organisation, this possibility should not stop you from making the recommendation in your report.

Potential Fraud	Controls currently in place	Risk to the organisation 1 = low, 5 = high	Implications	Improvement identified
1. Theft of assets	Physical access to the accounts department controlled by keypad but with common entry code	2	Loss of assets such as computers and possibly key data and information	Access code changed and only key staff have knowledge of it, non-current asset register kept
2. Overstatement of wages – wages clerk	None	4	Overpayment of wages to staff	All wages are countersigned on completion and system used to calculate wages based on hourly rates signed off by management

Sheffield City College Library

Potential Fraud	Controls currently in place	Risk to the organisation 1 = low, 5 = high	Implications	Improvement identified
3. Theft of cash from the office	Cash is kept in safe and office has keypad access	2	Loss of cash	See note 1 plus implement BACS payments for staff to eliminate use of cash
4. Theft of cash by overstating the weekly cheque	None	4	Loss of cash	Ensure if cash payments continue that cheque raised is double checked to cash required and countersigned by management
5. Theft of cheques	Cheque book kept in locked drawer – but control not always followed	4	Cheques could be used for own purchase / cash	Cheque book is kept in safe and log of cheques kept to ensure all accounted for
6. Overstatement of hours worked – stores supervisor	None	3	Overpayment of wages to stores staff	Staff should sign in and out of work and this should be used for wages calculations and countersigned by stores supervisor – a more comprehensive control, though perhaps not appropriate to Bayou would be a time keeping system based on staff clocking in and out of work
7. Theft of inventory from warehouse	None	4	Loss of inventory	Regular inventory checks and perhaps random checks on staff as they leave work

Potential Fraud	Controls currently in place	Risk to the organisation 1 = low, 5 = high	Implications	Improvement identified
8. Overpayment of supplier invoices	None	3	Increased costs	Accounting system should be used that matches invoices to purchase orders and goods received, this will produce reports on total payments for reconciliation. Also BACS payments for suppliers
9. Under recording of goods sold	None	3	Reduced revenue	Accounting system linked to tills could be initiated plus supervisory checks on tills. Also inventory checks to identify 'lost' inventory
10. Writing off customer debts	None	3	Increased costs	All debts written off must be authorised by business owner
11. Theft of cash / cheques from the mail	Cash and cheques received are written into day book	2	Lost cash / cheques, reduced revenue	Cash and cheques received are double checked by additional staff
12. Theft of cash / cheques from the tills	None – tills are not reconciled until the following day	3	Lost cash / cheques	Staff are paid an additional 30 minutes at the end of the day and reconcile their own tills before leaving work
13. Theft of cash from tills – petty cash / incidental expenses	Receipt is placed in till for items purchased	3	Lost cash / increased costs	Petty cash system implemented and controlled by accounting team

Potential Fraud	Controls currently in place	Risk to the organisation 1 = low, 5 = high	Implications	Improvement identified
14. Theft of wages – double paid	None if wages clerk is not available	2	Increased costs	Wages are paid by BACS or signed for only by that member of staff. Good records kept and any non-collected wages returned immediately to the safe with records.
15. Overpayment of suppliers	None if accounts payable ledger clerk is not available	2	Increased costs	Suppliers paid by BACS and centralised accounting system used. All supplier payments authorised with no manual ad-hoc payments made
16. Theft of wages – non staff member	None	2	Increased costs	Only the staff member can collect wages or must nominate a third party in writing. These records should be kept. Also pay staff by BACS instead.

3 Stolen cash receipts – clear procedures, and segregation of duties, controls for accepting cash payments and recording through the ledgers, also good controls for storage of cash and banking.

Overcharging on sales – sales systems such as bar coding that ensure prices are generated automatically. Authorisation of amendments to prices on system.

Inflating customer orders – segregation of duties and supervisory controls regarding matching orders to goods sent / handed to the customer.

Writing off debts – all debts require management authorisation to be written off.

Credit notes – all credit notes also require management authorisation before they can be processed on the system.

General controls include:

- Reconciliations of key customer accounts
- Spot checks of invoices to customer discounts
- Authorisation of all customer orders over a certain amount
- Not allowing customers to deal with only one member of staff

4   Ordering goods for own use – segregation of duties between ordering, booking goods into inventory and payments, plus supervision of each activity including appropriate authorisations.

Fictitious suppliers – management authorisation of all new suppliers added to the system and reconciliation of payments to invoices, also segregation of duties.

Paying amounts into own bank account – authorisation of all amendments to banking details on the system, segregation of duties   between amending details and processing payments.

Teeming and Lading – cash reconciliations, reconciling payments made to suppliers and invoices, segregation of duties

General controls include:

- Authorisation of all purchase orders

- Ordering from approved suppliers only

- Matching of goods received to purchase orders

- Matching of invoices to purchase orders and goods received

- Payments through BACS only and system generated to reflect invoices processed.

5   Ghost employees – reconciling the number of staff on the payroll to physical staff in the organisation plus good controls in connection with adding and removing staff from the payroll system.

Overstating overtime pay – clearly documented overtime rates for staff and management / supervisor authorisation of overtime hours worked.

Increasing hourly rate / salary – clearly documented pay rates plus all amendments to the hourly rate on the system should be countersigned by management. Perhaps also segregation of duties so only one of the payroll staff can amend rates, and the other reviews and gets authorisation for this from management.

False expense claims – all receipts included and travel checked for mileage and to diary. All claims authorised by management.

Keeping employees on the payroll – All resignations have to be officially documented and one member of the payroll staff is responsible for removing them from the system, the other checks this and management countersign.

Unofficial recruitment of new staff – All recruitments have to be officially documented and one member of the payroll staff is responsible for adding staff to the system, the other checks this and management countersign.

Examples of general controls include:

- Exceptions reporting – where the accounting system produces reports that highlight exceptions to the normal payroll such as particularly high payments, hours worked etc. These are checked and countersigned by management.

- Management countersigning the payroll staff's own pay.

- Spot checks on members of staff's pay to ensure it is accurate in relation to their pay scale and normal hours worked.

- No cash payments to staff

- Management checks on the payroll reports to look for duplicate bank details for example

- Rotation of payroll staff

CHAPTER 7   Cost Benefit Analysis and Completing your Report

1   Tangible costs associated with training might include:

- Cost of training course – say £500 per employee

- Cost of lost chargeable hours (as the staff will not be working on clients accounts) – 5 days x 7.5 hours per day = 37.5 hours at a chargeable rate of, say, £25 per hour = £937.5

- Travel expenses to the training provider – say £15 per day x 5 days = £75

2   Intangible costs might include:

- Other staff discontent as new staff are provided with training they did not have

- Loss of efficiency as new staff's induction is extended and therefore they are not available to work on clients

- Client dissatisfaction due to delays in completion of work due to staff not being available

3 Tangible benefits might include:

- Staff are better trained, so chargeable fee could be increased – from £25 to £30 per hour

- Fewer errors in work completed leading to less supervisor time spent on new staff's work and a reduction in having to amend work completed incorrectly – say 4 hours per week

Intangible benefits might include:

- Staff are better trained in basic knowledge so more motivated and efficient

- Staff morale improves as they feel valued due to the investment in training them

- Clients always see well trained and knowledgeable staff so organisation reputation is enhanced

Answers to chapter tasks

SAMPLE CASE STUDY AND REPORT

APPROACH TO PRODUCING THIS REPORT

As this example report is based around a Case Study it is essential to read the whole case through before deciding how to complete the report. Information required for different sections will be included throughout. A proposal for the report should then be produced and discussed with an assessor to ensure that the overall approach is correct and that a suitable part of the accounting system has been selected for review.

Once this proposal has been submitted and reviewed and discussed with the assessor then each section should be written using the exact same rules and format as required by a student completing the report based on their own work place. Each section, once completed, should then be submitted to the assessor for review and feedback.

The example that follows in this workbook was published by the AAT as one, complete word document. The actual case studies, for use in assessments, may be in a slightly different electronic format. They may consist of several documents which link together to provide a more realistic scenario. For example information on the staff employed by the organisation might take the format of CVs and appraisal documents. Students will be able to view these documents through a secure electronic platform on the AAT e portfolio and also print them if required.

WARNING!

Please note that the sample report that follows is an example only of how your finished report should look.

It should not be copied in any way into your report. You will need to testify that the report you submit is your own and unaided. If you submit a report with copied paragraphs from this sample answer your training provider could report you to the AAT Conduct and Compliance team.

AUTHENTICITY STATEMENT

This is a witness testimony that states that the work completed, to the writer's best knowledge, is your own, unaided and that the recommendations contained within it have been discussed.

It should be completed on headed paper, be signed and dated by your manager/assessor (see below) and have their full contact details.

If you have completed the project by reference to your work place then this statement **must** be completed by your manager and be on your organisation's headed paper. This effectively not only confirms that the work is your own and unaided, but also gives you permission to use your organisation as the basis of the project.

If you have completed the project based on an AAT Case Study then this must be completed by your assessor, on your training organisation's headed paper. In order for them to be able to testify that the work is your own, and unaided, it is essential that you communicate with them throughout the assessment process with project proposals and drafts.

The Sample Case Study – Bayou Stores Ltd

INTERNAL CONTROL & ACCOUNTING SYSTEMS

CASE STUDY

BAYOU STORES LIMITED

This sample case study is intended to indicate the type of situation that candidates will be presented with, and as such should be considered as an abridged version of those that will actually be used for live assessments.

Bayou Stores Ltd. is a large wholesale warehouse supplying a range of groceries, cleaning materials, and other household goods to small independent grocery stores. It was set up in 2008 by John Bayou, who having taken early retirement from his job as a fire fighter, used his pension and an inheritance to set up the business on the edge of Grantchester, a large industrial city. Besides the warehouse John, who is single, has only one hobby, which is golf. He usually spends all day Friday at the golf club – and other than this, he works very long hours for the other six days of the week.

He employs 30 staff in the stores and three part-time staff in the small accounts department. You have just been employed to work as the senior accounts clerk and, as the only full-time staff member, to supervise the running of the office. The store is open seven days a week, and operates from 7am until 10pm, Monday to Friday and from 10am to 6pm on Saturday and Sunday; whilst the accounts department only opens from 9am until 5pm Monday to Friday.

The accounts department's office is located on the first floor, over the warehouse store, which occupies the whole of the ground floor of the building. Access to the office is by stairs or an elevator from the ground floor – and this access is often used by the public – as the toilet facilities for staff and customers are also located on the first floor. Once on this floor access to the accounts office is gained through a keypad code; the code for which is UOYAB (Bayou read backwards). This code is relatively common knowledge throughout the company as it is also the alarm code for the building, and is used by the warehouse store supervisors and manager when they close up in the evenings.

Once inside the accounts office the working area is open plan, and anyone inside has full access to all the working areas.

The first job John has asked you to do is to review the accounting system and particularly the effectiveness of its internal controls. You are then asked to make any recommendations for improvement which you feel are necessary. (John knows there are many weaknesses – but is uncertain as to how these should be managed).

To help you in this he has asked the accounts clerks to prepare some brief information about themselves; an overview of the accounting system; and also a list of events that have occurred over the previous few months. This information can be found below.

The current staff in the accounting office are:

JO DOYLE (WAGES CLERK)

Jo is 24 years old and has been working for the company for four months. She is employed as a wages clerk and prepares the wages and salaries for all staff, along with all the associated returns, on a two day a week basis on Wednesday and Thursday each week. She has a young child, Harry, who is three years old, and spends all her free time with him. Though she is willing to work some extra hours if needed she does not want to commit herself to any more permanent hours – as she would need to rearrange her child care. Jo gained her AAT NVQ level 2 in payroll four years ago – but has never progressed any further since due to the arrival of Harry.

GARY IDAWO (ACCOUNTS CLERK)

Gary is eighteen years old and has been working for Bayou Stores for just a year since he left the local 6th form college, with three GCSE Advanced 'A' levels, including one in accounting. His main responsibilities are as the accounts receivable (sales ledger) clerk and his duties include running all the trade credit accounts for the company. He works four days a week – and has chosen not to work on a Friday. This is because his main hobby is music, and he plays in a band every weekend – and Friday is his rehearsal day. He has had no formal accounting training, but was trained on-the-job by the previous accounts receivable clerk before she left the company. He has, however, expressed an interest in learning, and wants to increase his accounting skills – but is uncertain how to go about this.

MARION SMITH (ACCOUNTS CLERK)

Marion is 57 years old and has been employed at Bayou Stores for eight months. She has recently been widowed and decided she needed to return to work to supplement her income. Her main role is that of accounts payable (purchase ledger) clerk. She is employed on a part-time basis of five half days per week, and she often likes to work these together to save on her bus fares to work. So for the past few months she has been working all day Tuesday and Wednesday and a half- day on Thursday morning. She has several years experience in operating accounting systems , but has not worked in this area for over ten years, since she left her last role to care for her sick husband.

The current accounting office practices and systems are outlined below.

INFORMATION TECHNOLOGY SYSTEMS

There are three computers in the office, as John has provided one for every member of the accounts team. These are all run on a stand-alone basis, though they are all linked to the same printer. Because John had some knowledge of Microsoft Office Excel spreadsheets whilst he was in the fire brigade (as they use this as their inventory (stock) control system) – he has based the inventory (stock) system for Bayou Stores on this same method; and because of this the wider accounting system is also being run using Excel.

Two computers were purchased new when the company was established and are running on Windows Vista operating system; they are also loaded with Microsoft Office 2007 version (with a three user licence). Six months ago a further new computer was also purchased and loaded with Sage Payroll software to enable the payroll to be run in-house.

When the computer system was set-up a password was installed to protect the work. This is also UOYAB, as John uses the same security code for everything throughout the company because he feels this makes life easier.

WAGES AND SALARIES

Until six months ago the payroll was completed by the company accountants, Pearl & Johnson. However, this was beginning to become very costly, as the individual hours worked each week by staff are so variable that the payroll run was different every week, and the accountants charged for the time taken to complete this. John made the decision that the wages and salaries could be run in-house. For the first two months he used a temping agency (but again this was an expensive option) to operate this – until four months ago when Jo started working for the company.

All store staff are paid weekly, in cash, and pay packets are available from the store manager from 8am on a Friday morning. The office staff and store manager are paid monthly, by cheque, on the last working day of each month.

Store staff are paid a basic rate of £7 per hour for the first 40 hours worked and time and a half for any hours over this from Monday to Saturday. Any hours worked on a Sunday are paid at double time. The store supervisors, of whom there are four, are also paid the same overtime premiums but based on a basic rate of £9 an hour.

The supervisors are responsible for preparing staff rotas for their own departments to ensure that there is adequate staff coverage for all of the opening hours. Most of the warehouse staff are willing to work overtime – so this does not usually create any problems. Once the week has finished, the completed rotas are given to Jo who uses them to calculate the amount of hours that the individual store staff have worked.

Jo prepares the payslips from this information on a Wednesday, calculating manually any overtime payments due, and any Sunday working. From this, she calculates how much cash needs to be drawn from the bank and uses the company cheque book (which is kept locked in Marion's desk) to prepare a cheque ready for John's signature. On a Thursday she then prepares the pay packets, which are stored in the office safe for the store manager to collect, (though often it is the supervisors who actually do this), and to hand out to the staff the following day. Any pay packets not given out are returned to the office safe and remain there until collected by the relevant member of staff.

Only Statutory Sick Pay (SSP) is paid to the warehouse store staff, but the office staff are salaried and are allowed four weeks contractual sick pay per year.

John has always trusted his workforce completely and there is no requirement, or system in place, for either store or office employees to sign in when they arrive or leave work.

ACCOUNTS PAYABLE (PURCHASE LEDGER)

All inventory (stock) is purchased on credit terms from a very wide range of suppliers. This is John's main role and he does enjoy spending time researching new stock lines, and also meeting the sales staff from different suppliers. He has a favourite group of suppliers he tends to use, mainly because the sales staff from these treat him to an occasional game of golf.

All inventory (stock) levels are maintained on the Excel spreadsheets. These have been set up to show suppliers; cost prices; selling prices; profit margins; and re-order levels and quantities. Marion has worked on Excel previously, but this was over ten years ago – and whilst she is competent at inputting data she sometimes struggles with anything beyond this.

Suppliers are paid at the end of the month in which their invoice is received, as long as funds are available. However, due to the current credit crunch some suppliers are now beginning to request payment earlier, within thirty days of the date of invoice, and this is beginning to cause John some concern.

All suppliers are paid by cheque. These are completed by Marion, and the only authorised signatory is John. The cheque book is stored in a locked drawer in Marion's desk in the accounts office.

ACCOUNTS RECEIVABLE (SALES LEDGER)

Gary is responsible for the running of this function. Whilst many customers do pay cash for their goods, over fifty per cent take extended credit terms. When Gary first started at Bayou Stores, anyone who applied for a credit account was accepted. However, he realised that this was not good practice and he now uses a credit reference agency to ensure that potential new credit customers have no history of poor payments. Other than this check any new customer who applied is automatically granted an unlimited line of credit.

All new credit accounts are set up on the first day of the month and Gary often works extra hours on this day to ensure this task is completed. All sales orders are received by the warehouse store staff for processing and after completion are passed to the accounts department the next morning, so that Gary can prepare the invoices and enter these in the accounts. Gary has designed a form in Microsoft Office Word which he uses as a pro forma for invoicing.

Bayou Stores offers sixty days credit to all their customers, and Gary is responsible for ensuring payment occurs. The policy on this is that once payment is seven days overdue Gary will telephone the customer. If payment is not received within seven days of the telephone call, then a 'stop' will be placed on the account and that customer is then not allowed any more goods or credit until payment has been made for any invoices more than sixty days old. Gary allows two half days per month for the task of telephoning customers who are late in paying; drawing the information from an aged receivables (debtors) control listing which has been set up on the Excel system to indicate customers whose accounts are outstanding for more than sixty days.

CASH AND BANKING

Gary opens the mail every morning and sorts through it. Any cash or cheques received from customers are entered manually into a day book to record the receipt, which is then used to update the accounts. The cheques and cash are then placed in the office safe until a banking day.

At the end of every day, all cash and cheques are removed from the tills, leaving a float of £100 cash in each till for the start of the next day. The principle is that the till should be balanced to ensure that the cash content is correct – but during the week this does not happen as the store closes at 10pm – and the supervisors feel that they should not be asked to do an extra job at this time of evening.

Therefore common practice is that all cash (except for the till floats) and cheques are removed and bagged as takings from individual tills before being stored in the safe in the accounts office.

Banking is carried out on a Monday and Thursday, and this is normally Gary's job which he does during his lunch break. The Thursday banking of cash is often lower as John has now started to reduce the cheques drawn for wages by the amount of cash available in the office safe on a Thursday morning. His idea is that any cash available can be used to supplement the making up of the wages to reduce the amount of cash needed to be drawn from the bank.

There is no petty cash system as such. If cash is needed for any incidental expenses, this is taken from the till floats and a note put in the till to cover this.

DIARY OF EVENTS FOR THE LAST THREE MONTHS

OCTOBER 20X0

One Tuesday, David Singh, a worker from the warehouse store, who has been off ill for five days, came into the office to collect his wages for the previous week, which he had not received due to his illness. His supervisor sent him upstairs to the accounts office, but even after a thorough search of the office safe, and then the office itself, the pay packet could not be found.

David was naturally annoyed at this and Gary tried to help. As Jo was not at work that day, and no-one else could operate the Sage payroll system it was not known how much David was owed. Gary decided that the rota said David was due to work 45 hours that week and so calculated his pay accordingly as:

35 x £7 plus 5 x £14 (Sunday working) plus 5 x £10.50 for overtime. Therefore he thought David was due £367.50 – so he gave him this amount of cash from the safe.

Later in the month Gary caught flu and was off work ill for two weeks. He therefore did no credit control work during this time. Marion worked one day extra a week to cover his work – but could not manipulate the data, or access the pivot table on the Excel spreadsheet that Gary uses to highlight outstanding payments.

In an unheard of incident John has taken the last five days of the month off to attend a golfing tournament he has been invited to by a supplier. However, this was a last minute invitation – and he only informed the accounts staff by telephone as he was on his way to the airport. He knew that he would need to pay suppliers during this time, and also staff wages – so he went to the office at 6am and signed a cheque book full of blank cheques to cover this. He had taken his spare keys with him, so was surprised when he discovered Marion's desk drawers unlocked.

On the last Friday of the month, Marion called into the office to pick up her salary cheque. As no one was about, and she knew that Jo had prepared these earlier in the week, she helped herself to this from Jo's desk drawer.

NOVEMBER 20X0

John told the accounts staff that after a telephone conversation with the bank manager he was very concerned over the size of the company overdraft and he had been informed that this must be reduced over the next four months.

He sat down with Gary to review the amounts owed by customers and was surprised to discover that more than twenty small retailers, who all are very good customers, owed more than £75,000 each. It became clear that they all take advantage of the full sixty day credit terms given by Bayou Stores and only make the minimum payment due, at the very end of this period. During this meeting Gary asked John about undertaking some accounts training, and John says he was very happy for him to do this, and would be willing to pay for it, if Gary could locate a suitable course.

On the first Monday in the month an irate supplier again telephoned the accounts office regarding late payments, and threatening to withdraw Bayou Stores credit facility. As Marion was not at work, Gary took the call and promised the supplier that the cheque would be in the mail that evening. He knew where the cheque book was kept, and that the drawer was often left unlocked; he thought he could complete the cheque and ask John to sign it and send it to the supplier immediately. However, he discovered that there was still a blank cheque which had already been signed by John during his golfing break, so he completed this and mailed it to the supplier to ensure they are satisfied. He was subsequently busy that week and so forgot to inform Marion of his actions – and as each accounts staff member only normally works on their own computer, he did not update the accounts payable system.

On the second Friday in the month the telephone in the accounts department was ringing incessantly. At lunch time Stevan Teery, a warehouse store supervisor, went into the accounts office to answer it – only to hear from a credit controller in a supplier company, who was chasing up an invoice that had not been paid within their thirty day terms. Stevan could only try and placate the supplier, and take a message for the accounts office staff.

The following week, five warehouse staff complained to Jo that their wages were wrong. They had been asked to work extra hours to cover staff sickness, but this had not been marked on the rota sheets, and therefore they had been underpaid for the extra hours they worked. Equally it meant that the two staff who were off ill, had been overpaid for these hours (but they have not reported this to the accounts department).

BPP
LEARNING MEDIA

DECEMBER 20X0

Jo had booked two weeks holiday over Christmas, as she wanted to spend this time with Harry. As she knew that she is the only member of staff who can operate the Sage payroll system she decided to complete three weeks pay packets on the same date – all based on the hours worked in the current week. She completed the pay packets and placed them in the safe, informing the supervisors that Gary will give them out on the correct Friday –and that any over or under payments will be adjusted during the following week after she has returned to work.

On the last Monday in the month a warehouse store worker, Matthew Perkins, came into the office to complain. Unbeknown to the other warehouse store staff he was having matrimonial problems, had recently left his wife to live with his girlfriend, and had taken a few days holiday last week for this move. His wife was aware that he was on holiday and had turned up at Bayou Stores and asked the supervisor for his pay packet saying that he was too busy to call in for it. As the supervisor knew his wife, (he had met her with Matthew at the staff Christmas party last year) he had handed her Matthew's pay packet without question – leaving Matthew with no money for the week.

TASKS

Complete a business report to John Bayou. This should be approximately 4000 words long, and should cover the following tasks:

Task 1

Complete a review of the accounting system

This can be of the complete system or of one or more of the accounting functions, depending on your findings – but must specifically cover the following areas:

1 Record keeping systems - the purpose of financial reports, and the suitability of the organisation's current reports to meet organisational needs. (EAS 1.2 & PIC1.2)

2 Internal systems of control – identify how internal control supports the accounting system and the types of internal control in place, and any controls that are missing. (PIC2.4, PIC3.2 & EAS 1.4)

3 Fraud - causes of fraud, common types of fraud, methods used to detect fraud and potential areas for fraud within the organisation (EAS 1.4, PIC2.2 & PIC2.3, PIC 3.1)

4 Working methods/practices -including the use of appropriate computer software, and the operating methods in terms of reliability, speed and cost effectiveness (PIC 3.4 & EAS 1.5)

5   Training (PIC 3.3) – Identify how training is or can be used to support staff.

The review should cover all aspects of the assessment criteria, as mapped above, when it can naturally be introduced into the report. If it cannot be covered in the report then it can be covered within a written explanation included in the appendix.

Whilst a SWOT analysis may be a good starting place, this should not be placed in the body of the report

Task 2

Identify weaknesses and make recommendations for improvement

- Once the review of the system has been completed the weaknesses that have been identified should be clearly explained along with their impact upon the organisation. (EAS 1.3 & PIC 3.1).

- For every weakness that has been identified there should be a recommendation made to attempt to improve the situation. (EAS 2.1 & PIC 2.4 & PIC 3.2)

The recommendations should concentrate on the effect that the changes would have both on the organisation, and on individual members of staff. (EAS 2.2 & PIC 1.5). They may also highlight training needs or aids to improve staff performance. (EAS 2.3 & PIC 3.3).

Task 3

Prepare a Cost Benefit Analysis

- At least one of the recommendations made should be subject to a cost benefit analysis. Whilst not all benefits are quantifiable all costs are – and students should make any necessary assumptions or 'guesstimates' to allocate costs to such items as time, unknown salaries, or any other unknown expense involved in the recommended changes.

- All benefits should be identified, included those which cannot be allocated a financial figure. This can include such things as improved customer relationships, improved documentation systems or staff morale (though this could be allocated a financial benefit as improving staff turnover cuts recruitment costs). (EAS2.4)

Note on Appendices: Any charts and diagrams or supporting evidence should be included here and cross -referenced within the text. Any appendices included should be referred to in the main body of the report – or in the case of supporting statements to cover missing assessment criteria, mapped and cross - referenced to a copy of the unit standards.

The Sample Report - Bayou Stores Ltd

Bayou Stores Limited

A report analysing the Internal Controls in place and Evaluating the Accounting Systems

Student Name:

AAT Registration Number:

I testify that the following report is my own unaided work and a true reflection of the organisation.

Signed: **Dated:**

Contents:

1. Terms of Reference
2. Executive Summary
3. Methodology
4. Introduction to the Organisation
5. The Accounts Department
6. Review of the Accounting System
7. Internal Control and Analysis of Fraud
8. Recommendations to Improve
9. Cost Benefit Analysis

Appendices:

1. Organisation chart
2. SWOT analysis
3. Fraud Matrix
4. Technical Notes
5. Mapping sheet

Word count: 4253

1. **Terms of Reference**

   1.1. This report investigates the accounting system in place within Bayou Stores Limited (Bayou) with regard to making recommendations to improve the system and the controls in place to protect it and make it less exposed to fraud.

   1.2. As part of the investigation into the system, this report also looks at the organisation as a whole, and the information needs it has from the system. It also investigates the key stakeholders of the organisation, both internal and external.

   1.3. The report also analyses the recommendations made in terms of the costs and benefits to Bayou and analyses the potential for fraud in terms of the risk to the organisation.

   1.4. Finally the report has been prepared to cover the requirements of the Internal Controls and Evaluating Accounting Systems Paper that is part of the AAT Level 4 Diploma in Accounting.

2. **Executive Summary**

    2.1 This report analyses the internal controls within the accounting systems of Bayou and makes recommendations to improve them. The key findings are that a centralised accounting system be installed within the accounts department, costing approximately £6,000. It is recommended that the accounts team be trained to use this system and procedural manuals and contingency plans be completed to enable staff to cover absence. A full Cost Benefit Analysis of all the recommendations is included in section 9 of this report.

    2.2. This will improve significantly the reporting of the organisation's finances and this in turn will improve credit control, payments to suppliers and relations with them, staff wages and morale. It will also improve controls and reduce the risk of fraud.

    2.3. The report also recommends that this be complemented by a BACS payments system so that suppliers and employees are paid direct into their accounts, reducing the use of cash and cheques hence improving controls.

3. **Methodology**

   3.1. To produce this report research was done using reference books and the Internet.

   3.2. A questionnaire was sent to the internal stakeholders to see what information they required from the accounts department and whether this information was being received in a timely manner.

   3.3. The existing accounting system was reviewed over a period of three months to enable a SWOT analysis to be produced.

   3.4. A fraud matrix was prepared to investigate the potential of fraud within the accounting system and to analyse the controls in place to prevent them.

4. Introduction to the Organisation

4.1. Bayou is a large, owner run wholesale warehouse supplying groceries, cleaning materials and other household goods to small independent grocery stores. It is a limited company, set up 2 years ago by John Bayou. John is the owner of the company and employs 30 staff in the stores and 1 full time and three part time staff in a small accounts department.

4.2. Bayou has grown since its set up and has recently brought the completion of the weekly and monthly wages and salaries in house where previously it was completed by a third party organisation. It has also recently employed the fourth member of the accounts team – a senior accounts clerk, with the role of managing the accounts department and personnel within it.

4.3. The organisation has a relatively flat structure, with two staff reporting to the owner and then further supervisors for the store staff. An organisation chart is included as Appendix 1 to this report.

4.4. The accounts system in use is a decentralised system consisting of three stand alone computers. The inventory control system is based around an Excel spreadsheet and the payroll system is run on Sage Payroll. The same password is used to protect the accounts departments work as is used on the keypad to enter the room.

4.5. **External regulations affecting the organisation:**

4.5.1. The Company's Act 2006 – this sets out the way in which financial statements should be prepared

4.5.2. UK Accounting standards – these further define the policies and approaches to the preparation of accounting statements that the organisation must take. They are either known as Statements of Standard Accounting Practices (SSAPs) or Financial Reporting Standards (FRSs) depending on when they were issued.

4.5.3. International regulations such as International Accounting Standards (IASs) and International Financial Reporting Standards (IFRSs), issued by the International Accounting Standards Board (IASB).

4.5.4. The Data Protection Act 1998 – This regulates how the organisation processes and stores sensitive information on customers, suppliers and employees. Bayou will need to ensure its systems are compliant with the Act or risk heavy penalties if data is found to be misused and/or stolen.

BPP
LEARNING MEDIA

4.5.5.   Late payment law – as set out in the Late Payment of Commercial Debt (Interest) Act 1998 the organisation will need to ensure that it does not delay payments to suppliers beyond acceptable periods.

4.5.6.   Health and safety legislation – as set out in a variety of legislation Bayou will need to comply with various health and safety principles and policies including having nominated and trained first aiders and safe working practices for staff.

4.5.7.   Food safety regulations – Bayou supplies groceries to customers and these will be affected by a variety of food hygiene regulations regulated by the Food Standards Agency.

4.6. Bayou – key external stakeholders

4.6.1.   Customers – the customers of Bayou are owners of small independent grocery stores who are purchasing wholesale goods to stock their stores. Their primary concern will be that they are provided with a good service at a low cost. They will also be interested in good credit terms with the organisation. Financial information required will include price lists.

4.6.2.   Suppliers – Suppliers to the organisation will be the manufacturers or importers of the goods it sells on to the grocery stores. There include a range of groceries, cleaning materials and other household goods. Suppliers will be concerned with prompt payments for the goods supplied. Financial information required will include information to enable them to decide whether to provide credit to Bayou.

4.6.3.   Bank manager – the bank of Bayou is a key stakeholder as the organisation has a large overdraft at present. If the overdraft has to be repaid then this will affect the cash flow of the organisation and potentially its ability to continue as a going concern. The bank will require financial accounts.

5. The accounts department

5.1. Bayou has an accounts team that are situated on the first floor, above the warehouse. There is open access to the floor as it also contains toilets used by customers. There is keypad access to the office itself, using a common code in use throughout the organisation.

5.2. All staff working within the organisation can access the office and do so to liaise with the accounting team, for example warehouse staff that wish to query their wages, and the owner to discuss the accounts or to sign cheques.

5.3. The purpose of the accounts department is to complete all activities relating to the production of the accounts including sales and purchase ledger and payroll. Due to some of the identified weaknesses there is little management accounting activity or cash flow forecasting. An organisation chart is included in appendix 1.

5.4. **The accounts department – key internal stakeholders**

5.4.1.   John Bayou, owner – as the owner of the business John will have a key interest in its success and will require various types of information including the final accounts. John will be concerned with the profit of the organisation, looking at turnover and also costs.

5.4.2.   Wages clerk –responsible for the preparation of the wages and salaries of staff. The clerk works two days per week and has an NVQ 2 in payroll.

5.4.3.   Accounts clerk 1 – The accounts clerk responsible for accounts receivable (sales ledger) runs all trade credit accounts for the organisation, working four days per week. The clerk has an accounts A level but no formal training and was trained on the job by the previous clerk.

5.4.4.   Accounts clerk 2 – The accounts clerk responsible for accounts payable (purchase ledger) works five half days per week. The clerk has several years experience in operating accounting systems but this was ten years ago. The clerk is relatively new to this role.

5.4.5.   Senior accounts clerk – a recent appointment the senior accounts clerk is responsible for managing the accounting team and systems and producing this report investigating the weaknesses of the accounts systems, with a focus on the payroll system, and making recommendations to improve them.

5.4.6. Stores staff – the stores staff are key stakeholders that interface with the customers of Bayou. They are primarily interested in good working conditions and pay. This includes good controls within the payroll system so that they are paid accurately and on time. They also require accurate inventory information from the accounts team.

6. Review of the accounting system

6.1. This report analyses the accounting system in place within Bayou and makes recommendations to improve it.

6.2. The weaknesses have been identified with the aid of a SWOT analysis – see appendix 2. This section also investigates the system within the context of the financial reports the accounts system should provide to stakeholders and whether it is suitable to meet their, and the organisation's, needs.

6.3. Working methods and practices

6.3.1. The systems in Bayou's accounts department consist of three stand alone computers, each operating independently of each other. The accounting and inventory system operates within Excel and the payroll system uses Sage Payroll to calculate the weekly and monthly wages and salaries. Invoices to customers are completed on a word document.

6.3.2. All work within the system is password protected, using a common password throughout the organisation.

6.3.3. Weaknesses in the working methods and practices within the systems at Bayou are detailed in the SWOT analysis in Appendix 2 as:

- Most staff are part time and there is no requirement in place for them to all be in the office at the same time. This can lead to a lack of communication and inefficiencies if they are trying to complete each other's work.

- As each system is independent of each other there is no training or cover for each of the roles within the organisation.

- There is no centralised reporting of the accounts due to different systems in use – this has led to an incomplete picture on the financial position of the organisation, especially in relation to cash flow.

- Many of the current working methods rely on manual systems, especially if the staff member who usually completes that work is absent. This could lead to errors and also a failure to inform the correct staff member when work has been carried out on their behalf.

- The current systems are slow for staff to use, not all are trained effectively and due to this they will not be cost effective. Manual systems and completion of information through Excel and Word can also lead to errors in data.

- There seems to be no back-up taken of the system, putting the organisation at risk of losing key data if the systems failed.

- There is a lack of planning in the work of staff which could lead to errors and inconsistencies.

6.4. Record keeping systems

6.4.1. Weaknesses in the record keeping system were identified as part of the SWOT analysis in appendix 2 as:

- There is no cover for staff when absent, so often urgent work is completed manually and no record kept or passed to staff.

- Payroll is calculated manually, which could result in errors.

- A reliance on Excel and Word for record keeping, especially with untrained staff, can lead to errors and inefficiencies. The Excel system in place is advanced and other staff can not use it. Errors could go unnoticed and be built into the spreadsheet.

- Petty cash is not recorded correctly and cash is taken from tills.

- When the tills are closed at the end of the day there is no recording of balances of cash / cheques etc.

- Payments have been made to suppliers on an ad-hoc basis and not recorded effectively.

- Warehouse staff hours are recorded on rotas which have been incorrect leading to incorrect wages paid. This is not an appropriate record keeping system.

- Wages have been completed in advance and therefore were not accurate.

- Cheques are not accounted for and signed for so there are incomplete records as to what they have been used for.

6.5.5. Training

6.5.1. The SWOT analysis in appendix 2 analyses the weaknesses within the system with regards to training as follows:

- Staff are not trained in accounting. This leads to a lack of knowledge about general controls and procedures in place plus a lack of ownership regarding the systems. If trained and qualified they would naturally take more responsibility for their work.

- Staff are often unable to use the current systems in place due to a lack of training in them. For example the pivot tables in the Excel spreadsheets. This can lead to further errors.

7. Internal controls and analysis of fraud

7.1. Internal systems of control

7.1.1. Within Bayou controls are very informal. Reliance is often based on trust. Formal internal controls will support the accounting system and reduce the possibility of fraud occurring.

7.1.2. The SWOT analysis in appendix 2 analyses the weaknesses with the system as:

- Cash – there are few controls regarding the use of cash within the organisation. Tills are not counted, cash is used to pay wages which are calculated manually, there is no double check of the wages when completed etc.

- Cheques – the current control in place is inadequate and also found to be not working as the desk drawer where the cheque book is kept has been found unlocked. Blank cheques are also signed and left with staff.

- Authorisation – there are no authorisation procedures in place. All cheques have to be signed by the owner and so blank signed cheques are left when he is absent. Wages are not authorised effectively and are calculated from staff rotas that could be incorrect.

- Counter-signatures – cash wages are not double checked and countersigned to prevent errors / fraud.

- Passwords / access – one common password is used throughout the organisation including to access the accounts office and systems. Any member of staff could use this password.

- Credit control – the only current control in respect of granting credit to customers is to check with a credit reference agency.

- New suppliers / customers - there are no controls in place before new suppliers and customers are added to the systems.

- Petty cash – no control system is in place.

- Collection of wages – there are no controls in place for who can collect staff wages. Wages are not signed for.

7.2. Analysis of fraud

7.2.1.   Although there is no evidence of fraud having taken place in Bayou there are many possible frauds that could occur within the system and appropriate controls should be in place to prevent them.

7.2.2.   The SWOT analysis in appendix 2 analyses the weaknesses with the system as:

- The use of cash to pay wages could lead to the theft of cash.

- The use of cash to pay wages could lead to the payroll staff colluding with weekly staff and adding more cash to the pay packet than the amount earned or shown on the wages slip.

- Cheques are not stored securely, so could be stolen and used fraudulently.

- Cheques are signed and left blank for staff to use when the owner is absent. This increases the risk of fraudulent use.

- There are no controls re new suppliers and so staff could defraud the organisation by setting up a bogus supplier and making payments to it.

- There are no controls re new customers and so staff could defraud the organisation by setting up a bogus customer.

- There is a working practice of taking cash from tills rather than a formal petty cash system – this could lead to staff taking cash for own use.

7.2.3.   Each of these potential frauds, the current controls in place, and the recommendations to improve can be found within a fraud matrix in appendix 3. This matrix also includes the level of risk to the organisation.

8. **Recommendations to improve**

8.1. There are many recommendations that can be implemented to improve the weaknesses identified above and in appendix 2.

8.1.1. The first is that a centralised accounts package be purchased. This will be used to complete the sales and purchase ledger, the payroll and the other financial transactions. This will need the computers currently in use within the department to be networked. This would enable the organisation to have central accounting records. Staff would be motivated by using a common system that is effective and provides them with the appropriate information that they require to complete their work. It would also lead to fewer errors in manual calculations, benefitting both staff and the organisation.

8.1.2. Staff must be fully trained to use the system so that they can operate it effectively and efficiently. This will improve their morale and make them more efficient.

8.1.3. The system should also be properly backed up with procedures for who is responsible for completing this at the end of each working day. This will ensure the organisation does not lose key information in the event of a system failure.

8.1.4. Staff should also receive formal accounting training if requested. This will motivate them and also provide them with a much better understanding of the need for controls and examples of controls that should be in place. This will in turn benefit the organisation.

8.1.5. There should also be a review of staff hours and days to ensure that staff are in at appropriate times plus a formal procedure in place to train staff in second roles to cover for each other's absence. This will improve morale as staff are better trained and have more variety in their work plus benefit Bayou as there will be appropriate cover in place.

8.1.6. This could be strengthened by the completion of procedural manuals to explain how to operate the systems. This will aid the department in the event of training new staff if required.

8.1.7. The door code and the passwords to access the system must be changed and all staff of Bayou informed of the need to have effective controls in place. This will ensure the risk of fraud is reduced.

8.1.8. As part of the centralised accounts system a payments system, by BACS, should be implemented so that suppliers and staff wages are paid direct into bank accounts and the use of cash and cheques reduced. This could include monthly wage payments for all staff and will significantly reduce the risk of fraud together with the risk of theft of cash and errors in calculations.

8.1.9. An effective petty cash system should be implemented and petty cash recorded appropriately. This will benefit the organisation by reducing the risk of theft or poor recording of cash taken from the tills.

8.1.10. All tills must be counted and reconciled at the end of each working day – staff should be paid to stay back and complete this work. This will reduce the risk of fraud or errors and make till staff more accountable for the contents of their till, changing the culture to one more based on controls.

8.1.11. There should be controls in place to add new suppliers and customers to the accounts system, with authorisation only from the owner and/or the senior accounts clerk.

8.1.12. The cheque book should be kept locked in the safe and the system of signing blank cheques stopped. The senior accounts clerk could be added as a second signatory if required. This will ensure staff are happy that they can have cheques authorised in the event of the owner's absence but benefit Bayou by reducing the risk of fraud.

8.1.13. Further checks on customers should be completed before they are granted credit. This will benefit the organisation by reducing the risk of bad debts and ensuring that credit is only granted to customers who are likely to be able to pay their debts.

8.1.14. The centralised accounts system will enable full financial reports to be completed and this will enable both the owner and the senior accounts clerk to review all aspects surrounding the organisation's financial position, including aged debts analysis. This will ensure better planning of cash flows so that the current overdraft can be reduced and aged debts dealt with appropriately. It will also ensure that suppliers are paid promptly.. This will reduce the risk of suppliers putting Bayou on stop due to unpaid bills.

8.1.15. It is also recommended that the senior accounts clerk be responsible for the operation and management of the new system. Including the setting of appropriate password controls.

9. Cost benefit analysis

9.1. A cost benefit analysis of the recommendation to implement a centralised accounting system, and train staff appropriately on it, has been completed as follows:

9.2. Costs

9.2.1. An example system that Bayou could purchase would be a centralised accounts package such as *Accounts Professional* which has been specifically created for small to medium sized organisations. There are many such packages on the market and a full investigation should be completed to determine which bests suits the organisation. A package with a multi user licence would cost approximately £2,400. Whichever package is chosen it should be easy to use and come with user manuals and have help menus and drop down boxes to improve efficiency.

9.2.2. Bayou would also need to purchase an appropriate support package and this could cost an additional £1,000.

9.2.3. Appropriate training for staff is required If the accounts package purchased is one in common use then Bayou will be able to purchase places on open courses for staff, costing approximately £300-£500 per staff member. Bayou might also consider a tailored training course for all staff at once, to include partial set up of the system for Bayou's use, which would cost approximately £2,000.

9.2.4. There would also be an opportunity cost of the staff attending the training in that they would not be available to complete their work at Bayou.

9.2.5. The organisation also requires the appropriate equipment to network the computers and this could be completed either by cable or on a secure wireless network, and cost approximately £500 - £1,500. Cabling would be more reliable but create disruption to the office whilst being installed where as a wireless network would be quicker, but could lose connection on occasions.

9.2.6. Bayou would face some disruption whilst the system is installed and set up, although during much of this period staff can continue with the current manual systems. There will be a need to pay for additional staff time to enter data on customers, suppliers and employees into the system so that it is fully operational and it is anticipated that this could be completed within one week. This would require an additional 50 paid hours costing approximately £900.

9.2.7. A further cost the organisation should consider, but one harder to quantify, is that of staff discontent at a change to the current system. This might be staff within the accounts team who are unhappy with having to learn new working practices, increased controls and how to operate a new system. It might also include other employees, who see the increased controls in place as preventing them carrying out their work and unnecessary.

9.2.8. Finally there would be a cost of producing procedure manuals to ensure staff can use the system and also a rota for cover when staff are absent. This can be completed by the senior accounts clerk within their normal role and would take approximately 20 hours of their time.

9.3. Benefits

9.3.1. The benefits the system will bring are less tangible, so harder to value. Where it has been possible to quantify a benefit this has been done.

9.3.2. The first benefit to Bayou would be the completion of centralised reports showing the full financial position of the organisation. These can be reviewed on a regular basis by both the owner and the senior accounts clerk to ensure that cash flows are effectively managed. This will benefit the organisation by reducing overdraft fees. The reports produced would include:

- Income statement (profit and loss account)
- Statement of financial position (balance sheet)
- Aged debt analysis
- Forecast of statement of cash flows (forecast cash flow statement)
- Supplier payment reports
- Costs by cost centre / code
- Analysis of petty cash expenditure
- Payroll reports

9.3.3. An aged debt report can be produced to strengthen the system of chasing overdue debts and ensuring customers who have not paid are put on stop quickly. This will prevent customers from taking advantage of the current lax controls. It has been calculated that approximately £2,000 per year of bad debts would be saved.

9.3.4. Forecasts of statements of cash flows (or cash flow statements and forecasts) will enable the owner and senior accounts clerk to estimate the cash inflows and outflows to the organisation, manage cash balances more effectively and reduce the overdraft and related fees. It will also assist with the planning of any significant cash expenditure.

9.3.5. The payroll will be accurately produced when required, with the benefit of the system being up to date on payroll rules and regulations such as tax rates. This will produce a benefit of more accuracy, fewer queries and increased efficiency of staff time. It is estimated that the system will speed up the completion of the payroll by approximately 4 hours per month.

9.3.6. There will be less danger from a system breakdown with appropriate back up of a central system. If one computer were to fail then the other staff could continue working and a support agreement would ensure that if the main system failed it could be operational again as quickly as possible with less risk of lost or corrupted data.

9.3.7. Another benefit would be improved supplier relations – reports on supplier payments due could be run and suppliers paid on time. This could also benefit the credit terms and conditions that suppliers grant Bayou, further improving cash flow.

9.3.8.   A further benefit is the significant reduction in the risk of fraud and improvement of controls within the system together with improved cost control. Central reports will assist both the owner and the senior accounts clerk with analysing payments and wages and identifying where costs are higher than expected. Due to current poor controls it is not known if Bayou has suffered from fraudulent activities so benefits are hard to evaluate.

9.3.9.   A benefit would also be improved morale of staff. The accounts team would benefit from training, including formal accounts training as requested and this would improve their efficiency and effectiveness as well as morale. Better motivated staff should result in lower staff turnover and also improved commitment to the organisation.

9.3.10. The morale of the non-accounting staff would be improved by the timely completion of accurate wages.

9.3.11. A final benefit would be that Bayou would then be able to comply with regulations such as the Data Protection Act 1998 with good, secure storage of its data and information.

Appendix 1 – Organisation chart

Appendix 2 – SWOT analysis

Strengths	Weaknesses
■ An open plan accounts office ensures that when staff are in and working with each other they can communicate freely and cover each other's work when absent.	■ As most accounts staff are part time there are often occasions when no one is in the office. As all staff can access the office and the accounts system with common passwords there is a risk of lack of control. There will also be issues concerning communication between staff as they are not all in the office at the same time.
■ The cheque book is kept in a locked desk in the office – but see weaknesses.	■ Stand alone computers with no central system means that the system does not produce central, standard reports for key stakeholders
■ Current inventory system has good detail included	■ Staff, as a whole, are not qualified in accounting which poses a risk of errors and relaxed controls and also a lack of accountability.
■ Credit reference agency used to decide whether to grant credit	
■ Credit control procedures in place	■ There appears to be a lack of planning in the work of the accounting team, highlighted by the fact that when the payroll was first brought in house a temping agency was contracted to run it for the first two months. This could have led to errors and inconsistencies in the work, and the hand over of the system to the payroll clerk once employed.
■ Controls re: cash and cheques coming into the office – manual day book then accounts.	
■ Staff seem keen to improve systems – Accounts receivable clerk has implemented some initiatives.	
■ Cash movement is reduced by using to make up wages.	■ Stores staff are paid in cash which poses a risk of theft
	■ Office staff are paid by cheque – the frequent use of cheques can lead to the risk of cheques being stolen and fraudulently used.
	■ Manual calculation of weekly payroll with no secondary check is a weakness as it can lead to errors or fraudulent increases in staff pay.
	■ Cash is withdrawn to pay wages – as above, any use of cash poses a risk of theft.

	<ul><li>On at least one occasion the cheque book was accessed by other members of staff as the draw it is kept in was found to be unlocked.</li><li>Staff are not trained in Excel and could make errors</li><li>No further check on new credit customers other than credit reference agency</li><li>Manual completion of invoices, on Word, could lead to errors.</li><li>Cash is not counted when removed from the tills on weekdays.</li><li>No petty cash system – so no control on cash taken from tills.</li><li>No contingency planning – staff able to take on each other's roles when absent.</li><li>Staff can not use each other's systems.</li><li>No control on authorisation – signing of blank cheques to cover absence.</li><li>No controls on payments to customers.</li><li>Payments to suppliers are made without checking systems, or informing other staff.</li><li>Lack of controls on staff hours have led to incorrect rotas and staff pay.</li><li>Three weeks pay packets completed in one go – this is a weakness as too much cash was in the office.</li><li>Wages should be completed correctly, not in advance and adjusted later.</li><li>Pay is handed to staff family members, there is no control that it should only be handed to staff / others with permission.</li></ul>

Opportunities	Threats
▪ There is an opportunity to use one central accounts system on networked computers which will ensure that there is better cover for work when staff are absent and better reporting of key financial data to relevant stakeholders.	▪ Having the accounts prepared on Excel poses a risk that errors can be made in the spreadsheets that will not be easily identified, and therefore the inventory and accounting information may be incorrect.
▪ There is an opportunity to train staff in accounting and also in the systems they use, making them much more aware of the controls and procedures they should be operating with and also more efficient.	▪ There is a threat to the office and its systems by the common use of one password across the organisation – any staff who wanted to could access the office and the accounting systems.
▪ There is an opportunity to train staff in each other's roles – perhaps with a back-up member of staff for each. This could motivate staff and also ensure cover during absence.	▪ The lack of formal procedures and control in respect of accounts receivable and payable has led to an overdraft the bank has asked to be repaid. This is a cash flow threat to the organisation.
▪ There is an opportunity to outsource the payroll and internal audit functions to the company accountants.	▪ There appears to be no back-up taken of the current systems. This is a threat because, if the systems in use failed, key financial data would be lost.
	▪ Regulatory environment – this is constantly changing, for example potential changes to VAT rates. The accounting system needs to recognise these changes and react accordingly

Appendix 3 – Fraud Matrix

Potential Fraud	Current Control	Risk to the Organisation	Recommendation
The use of cash to pay wages could lead to the theft of cash.	Cash is kept in the safe	5 – High	Pay staff by BACS reducing the use of cash
The use of cash to pay wages could lead to the payroll staff colluding with weekly staff and adding more cash to the pay packet than earned and on the wages slip.	None – wages are not double checked or countersigned	5 – High	Either ensure a thorough check of wages calculated and cash included or pay staff by BACS as above.
Cheques are not stored securely, so could be stolen and used fraudulently.	Stored in locked drawer – but often found to be unlocked	4 – High	Store cheques in the safe only
Cheques are signed and left blank for staff to use when the owner is absent. This increases the risk of fraudulent use.	None	5 – High	Allow a second signatory for when absent and reduce use of cheques through BACS wages and payments.
There are no controls re new suppliers and so staff could defraud the organisation by setting up a bogus supplier and making payments to it.	None	3 – Medium	All new suppliers and customers should be entered to a central accounting system and authorised either by owner or senior accounts clerk

Potential Fraud	Current Control	Risk to the Organisation	Recommendation
There are no controls re new customers and so staff could defraud the organisation by setting up a bogus customer and purchasing goods from it.	None	3 – Medium	All new suppliers and customers should be entered to a central accounting system and authorised either by owner or senior accounts clerk
There is a working practice of taking cash from tills rather than a formal petty cash system – this could lead to staff taking cash for own use.	Receipts are left when cash is taken to purchase items	4 – High	Operate an effective petty cash system and ensure tills are reconciled at the end of each day

Key to risk
1 = Low, 3 = Medium, 5 = High

Appendix 4 – Technical Notes

If an assessment criterion is not covered in the report (or not to the depth required by the assessor), then this can be covered within a written explanation included in the appendix.

Where this is the case technical notes should be included in the appendices to the report to ensure that an area of the standards is covered in sufficient detail to clearly demonstrate competence.

Exactly what will be required by the technical notes will depend on every student and assessor plus the workplace vs. case study used to complete the report.

It should be noted that as these notes are in the appendices they do not contribute to the word count.

In the example of Bayou examples of appropriate technical notes might include:

1   **Income statement (profit and loss account)** – in the context of Bayou this would show the owner of the organisation the income or revenue received and the costs of the business. This could show profitability by month or by product depending on the detail required. This would assist the owner with making decisions and analysing the business and would highlight key costs such as bank interest. This would have led to an earlier understanding of the size of the overdraft. Once costs like these have been identified they then can be better controlled.

2   **Statement of financial position** (balance sheet) - in the context of Bayou this would show the assets and the liabilities of the organisation. It would also show details of the receivables (debtors) and payables (creditors) and allow the owner to have a regular and more accurate picture of these. This would help to highlight any issues with the size and/or management of payables and receivables.

3   **Fraud detection** – There are many ways to detect that fraudulent activities may be taking place. A small organisation would not have an internal audit department but control checks can still be planned and made on a regular basis. Management should also look for staff who appear to be living a wealthier lifestyle than their position in the organisation as this may suggest that fraud is taking place. Good management, supervision and procedures in place to protect cash and assets are all good controls to prevent and detect fraud.

4   **Impact of fraud** – Fraud is effectively theft from the owners of the business. The theft can be of assets such as inventory or equipment, of cash or of time. It could be that staff are using company time to complete personal activities. Fraud reduces the profitability of the organisation and can also lead to demoralised staff; who might be aware that fraud is taking place but are afraid to report it. Fraud can also lead to a culture of mistrust which is not a very effective working environment.

Appendix 5 – Mapping Sheet

Principles of Internal Control		
Learning Outcome	**Assessment Criteria**	**Paragraph Numbers**
1. Demonstrate an understanding of the role of accounting within the organisation	**1.1** Describe the purpose, structure and organisation of the accounting function and its relationships with other functions within the organisation	4.3 4.4 4.6 5.1 5.2 5.3 5.4 **Appendix 1**
	1.2 Explain the various business purposes for which the following financial information is required ■ income statement (profit and loss account) ■ forecast of cash flow (cash flow statement) ■ statement of financial position (balance sheet)	9.3.2 9.3.3 9.3.4 **Technical Note: 1, 2**
	1.3 Give an overview of the organisation's business and its critical external relationships with stakeholders	4.1 4.2 4.6 5.4
	1.4 Explain how the accounting systems are affected by the organisational structure, systems, procedures, and business transactions	4.4 8.1.1
	1.5 Explain the effect on users of changes to accounting systems caused by ■ external regulations ■ organisational policies and procedures	5.4 9.3.5 9.3.11 6.5

2. Understand the important and use of internal control systems	2.1 Identify the external regulations that affect accounting practice	4.5 9.3.5 9.3.11
	2.2 Describe the causes of, and common types of, fraud and the impact of this on the organisation	7.2 **Appendix 3**
	2.3 Explain methods that can be used to detect fraud within an accounting system	7.1 7.2 **Appendix 3**
	2.4 Explain the types of controls that can be put in place to ensure compliance with statutory or organisational requirements	8.1.1 8.1.6 8.1.11 8.1.13 8.1.14 **Appendix 3**
3. Be able to identify and use the appropriate accounting system to meet specific organisation requirements	3.1 Identify weaknesses in accounting systems ■ potential for errors ■ exposure to possible fraud.	**Appendix 2** 6.3 eg 6.3.3 6.4 6.5 7.1 7.2
	3.2 Explain how an accounting system can support internal control	8.1.1 8.1.4 8.1.8 8.1.9 8.1.10
	3.3 Identify ways of supporting individuals who operate accounting systems using ■ training ■ manuals ■ written information/help menus	6.5 8.1.2 8.1.4 8.1.6 8.1.9 8.1.12 8.1.14 9.2.3

	3.4 Explain the value and benefit to a specific organisation of different types of accounting systems and software packages	8.1 8.1.9 9.2.1 8.1.5

Evaluating Accounting Systems		
Learning Outcome	**Assessment Criteria**	**Paragraph Numbers**
1. Evaluate the accounting system and identify areas for improvement	1.1 Identify an organisation's accounting system requirements	4.4 8.1.2
	1.2 Review record keeping systems to confirm whether they meet the organisation's requirements for financial information	6.4
	1.3 Identify weaknesses in and the potential for improvements to, the accounting system and consider their impact on the operation of the organisation	**Appendix 2** 6.3 6.4 6.5 8.1
	1.4 Identify potential areas of fraud arising from lack of control within the accounting system and grade the risk	7.2 **Appendix 3**
	1.5 Review methods of operating for cost effectiveness, reliability and speed	6.3.3 6.4.1 9.2 9.3

2. Make recommendations to improve the accounting system	2.1	Make recommendations for changes to the accounting system in an easily understood format, with a clear rationale and an explanation of any assumptions made.	8.1
	2.2	Identify the effects that any recommended changes would have on the users of the system.	8.1.3 8.1.5 8.1.6 9.2.7 9.3.9
	2.3	Enable individuals who operate accounting systems to understand how to use the system to fulfil their responsibilities.	8.1.2 8.1.3 8.1.5 8.1.6 8.1.7 8.1.10 8.1.11 8.1.13 8.1.15
	2.4	Identify the implications of recommended changes in terms of time, financial costs, benefits, and operating procedures.	9.2 9.3

Sample case study and report

INDEX

Notes

Notes

Notes

REVIEW FORM

How have you used this Workbook?
(Tick one box only)

☐ Home study

☐ On a course_____

☐ Other _____

Why did you decide to purchase this Workbook?
(Tick one box only)

☐ Have used BPP Texts in the past

☐ Recommendation by friend/colleague

☐ Recommendation by a college lecturer

☐ Saw advertising

☐ Other _____

During the past six months do you recall seeing/receiving either of the following?
(Tick as many boxes as are relevant)

☐ Our advertisement in Accounting Technician

☐ Our Publishing Catalogue

Which (if any) aspects of our advertising do you think are useful?
(Tick as many boxes as are relevant)

☐ Prices and publication dates of new editions

☐ Information on Text content

☐ Details of our free online offering

☐ None of the above

Your ratings, comments and suggestions would be appreciated on the following areas of this Workbook.

	Very useful	Useful	Not useful
Introductory section	☐	☐	☐
Quality of explanations	☐	☐	☐
Chapter tasks	☐	☐	☐
Chapter Overviews	☐	☐	☐
Index	☐	☐	☐

	Excellent	Good	Adequate	Poor
Overall opinion of this Workbook	☐	☐	☐	☐

Do you intend to continue using BPP Products? ☐ Yes ☐ No

Please note any further comments and suggestions/errors on the reverse of this page. The author of this edition can be e-mailed at: paulsutcliffe@bpp.com

Please return to: Paul Sutcliffe, Senior Publishing Manager, BPP Learning Media Ltd, FREEPOST, London, W12 8BR.

REVIEW FORM (continued)

TELL US WHAT YOU THINK

Please note any further comments and suggestions/errors below.